NEXTGENERATION HEALTHCARE

NEXTGENERATION HEALTHCARE

Proven Secrets of Managing the Healthcare Value Chain
to Improve Outcomes and Reduce Costs

This publication is designed to provide accurate and authoritative information with regard to the subject matter covered. It is sold with the understanding that the publisher is not engaged in rendering legal, accounting or other professional advice. If legal advice or other expert professional assistance is required, the services of a competent professional person should be sought.

Published by AIL Press
Part of the Association for Insurance Leadership
A division of Bottom Line Solutions, Inc.
101 Creekside Crossing
Suite 1700 – Box 304
Brentwood, TN 370276
(615) 369-0618

Association for Insurance Leadership
  NextGeneration Healthcare: Proven Secrets of Managing the Healthcare Value Chain to Improve Outcomes and Reduce Costs / Various
    p.cm.
  1. Business. 1. Title
    ISBN 978-0-9882823-5-3 (paperback)
    ISBN 978-0-9882823-6-0 (hardcover)

Printed and bound in the United States of America

DEDICATION

This book is dedicated to the visionary and intrepid men and women who reject the benefits status quo to embrace the NextGen Benefits Revolution. You are helping employers reclaim control of their benefits spend and create true Healthcare Value Chains that deliver quality, affordable healthcare for their employees.

Table of Contents

Preface

The mission of the Association of Insurance Leadership (AIL) is to elevate the employee benefits industry, in part by providing and promoting collaboration and thought leadership.

What better way to fulfill the AIL mission than by publishing this remarkable collection of strategic insights, innovative strategies, and effective techniques to improve the quality of employees' healthcare while reducing the cost of that healthcare for both the employee and the employer. This information is willingly shared by the authors, who are leading business consultants and NextGen Benefits Advisers who daily are using the information between these covers to improve the benefits and the finances of their employer clients across the U.S.

The authors are NextGen Benefits Advisers, many members of the NextGen Benefits Mastermind Partnership, over 40 employee benefits firms from across the nation that are innovating to challenge the status quo in the employee benefits industry and in healthcare. These NextGeneration Benefits Advisers are in the vanguard of the industry, setting the standard for both quality of the benefits offered employees and the cost-effectiveness and sustainability of the benefits plan for employers.

The intended audience for this book are the organizational leaders who are responsible for both the benefits on which their employees depend and the large and ever-increasing benefit budget that, for most companies, rank in the top two or three line items on the P&L statement. The strategic insights and innovative strategies are intended for the C-level executives with the strategic and fiduciary responsibility for the benefits program. The proven techniques are intended for the benefits professionals in HR with the operational responsibility to implement and execute the benefits program.

Every day, the authors of this disruptive book are elevating the industry by providing better benefits at lower cost to employers and their employees. They are elevating the industry by raising the bar for other benefits firms in their market. This is the progressive, forward-thinking leadership that will move the employee benefits industry squarely into the 21st century.

The Association for Insurance Leadership is delighted and honored to present these NextGen Benefits strategies and techniques to the men and women with fiduciary and operational responsibility for benefits at their company.

Introduction

> "*The problem with healthcare costs isn't insurance. Stop proposing insurance solutions to a supply chain problem.*"
>
> —**Bob Gearhart, Jr.**, CEO,
> DCW Group, Youngstown, OH

Healthcare costs in the U.S. have risen every year since 1960 and, since 1999, these costs have exploded, increasing by 261 percent through 2016. Driven by rising healthcare costs, health insurance premiums are not far behind, growing by 213 percent during the same period.

As a result, employers that offer health insurance have been stuck in a real-life version of the Bill Murray film classic, "Groundhog Day," waking up every renewal season to another increase of their insurance premiums. As premiums rise and employers shift more of the costs to employees out of financial necessity, healthcare as an employee benefit is becoming unaffordable for employees and unsustainable for employers. And the health insurance companies and insurance brokers who maintain the status quo seem to have no answer to this seemingly intractable problem.

But answers—proven, effective answers—exist and are readily available. The authors of this book—innovative NextGen Benefits Advisers who have rejected the status quo in both benefits and healthcare—reveal many of those answers in the chapters that follow.

Most important, these NextGen Benefits Advisers debunk healthcare's Big Lie: that the C-Suite has no control over the cost of healthcare.

Despite what they've been told repeatedly for decades, CEOs and CFOs certainly can control healthcare costs. It shouldn't surprise these business leaders that rising healthcare costs are a result of mismanagement of the healthcare supply chain. Fortunately, NextGen Benefits Advisers are expert at applying supply chain strategies to build a true Healthcare Value Chain that delivers quality outcomes at fair and reasonable prices.

Even as healthcare's two middlemen—the insurance companies and brokers—continue to allow healthcare costs to increase unchecked by bringing insurance solutions to a supply chain problem, NextGen Advisers are reducing the year-over-year cost of healthcare for their employer clients, often by 20 to 40 percent or more in the first year. They are reducing costs in years two and three, as well. And NextGen Advisers are creating these remarkable results across the U.S., for employers large and small.

Equally important, by managing the Healthcare Value Chain for the CEO and CFO, NextGen Benefits Advisers are improving medical outcomes for employees and enhancing their benefits, even as they reduce the employer's benefits spend.

NextGen Benefits and the intrepid NextGen Benefits Advisers who are implementing them are bringing market discipline and supply chain strategies to the purchase of healthcare, creating affordable and sustainable NextGeneration Healthcare.

CHAPTER **ONE**

Healthcare's Big Lie

*How Healthcare's Middlemen
Have Deceived America's C-Suites
and Fleeced U.S. Business of Billions*

NELSON L. GRISWOLD

I n C-Suites across America, a quiet revolution is overthrowing
the tired and unsustainable Status Quo in employee benefits
and healthcare and providing a real and permanent solution to
the healthcare cost problem.

After years of enduring steep annual increases in the cost of
benefits, in 2017 the leadership of Garden State Engineering
Surveying and Planning (GSESP) in Maywood, NJ, reclaimed
control of its benefits spend and in 12 months lowered its
year-over-year healthcare costs by an eye-opening 26 percent.

In the second year of its new healthcare plan, GSESP used part of its cost savings to eliminate totally the $5,750 family deductible while keeping the same affordable weekly premium contribution, producing a healthcare plan that employees can afford with no risk of large out-of-pocket expenses to keep them up at night or prevent them from accessing the healthcare they need.

"We now have a phenomenal retention, recruiting, and employee satisfaction tool with savings on top of it!" said Gary Bender, GSESP's Executive Vice President and CFO.

GSESP began to reverse what widely is considered an immutable fact of business life when John Sbrocco of Questige Consulting, a NextGen Benefits Adviser, engaged Bender in a financial conversation about his company's benefits budget and strategy.

A CFO's Epiphany

"In talking to John, it became obvious that what was missing from my benefits process was me, as CFO," said Bender. He now works closely on benefits strategy with Sbrocco, who manages the firm's Healthcare Value Chain for Bender to improve outcomes and lower costs. Active in the organization, CFO Solution, Bender has openly shared his eureka moment and bottom-line success with other CFOs, many of whom are adopting the same set of "next" practices and are seeing very similar results.

Despite Bender's evangelical efforts, however, he and his converts remain rare exceptions. In the ongoing national battle to control the cost of healthcare, America's C-Suite has been conspicuously absent. And Bender is not the only C-Suite veteran to recognize that executives have been AWOL from the benefits discussion.

"I would make a class-action apology for all CEOs. We allowed the mess on the economic side of health care to happen," asserts John Torinus Jr., the now-retired CEO of Wisconsin-based manufacturer Serigraph, Inc., in his influential book, *The Company that Solved Health Care.* "CEOs should be embarrassed at how they have allowed health costs to run wild. They would not allow that to happen in any other part of their businesses."

But why has the C-Suite not been engaged in benefits management? What could have convinced otherwise savvy executives to ignore—and continue to ignore—what has metastasized into most companies' second or third largest P&L expense?

The Big Lie

"As a business executive, you have no control over the cost of healthcare. Healthcare costs—and your health insurance rates—will increase annually and there's nothing you can do about it."

This is the Big Lie that healthcare's middlemen—the health insurance companies (carriers) and their insurance broker accomplices—have been telling the C-Suite for decades.

This Big Lie is responsible for the most egregious, mass lapse of corporate fiduciary responsibility in the history of American business.

It may be surprising that almost every executive and business owner in America has fallen for the Big Lie that the buyer/payor has no ability to influence the cost of healthcare goods and services . . . when they ruthlessly manage their sourcing in every other part of their business. But as history has proven, a Big Lie repeated often enough and with conviction becomes accepted as Truth.

Believing the Big Lie that they had no control over their healthcare costs, the C-Suite understandably tagged their benefits spend an OpEx, stuck it in SG&A, and promptly ignored it in favor of items they could manage. Believing it was unmanageable from a cost perspective, executives delegated operational management of the benefits plan to a Human Resources line manager with no P&L responsibility.

And, by default, executives delegated the management of healthcare purchasing to their insurance carrier, mostly the big five known collectively as the BUCAHs (**B**lue Cross, **U**nitedHealthcare, **C**igna, **A**etna, **H**umana).

Over the past several decades, as putative stewards of companies' benefits spend, the BUCAHs "proved" the Big Lie that it is impossible to restrain the rising cost of healthcare.

"Medical Trend"

Despite frequent and regular announcements that they are working hard to control and reduce the cost of healthcare, the BUCAHs have failed dismally to stem the growth of healthcare costs, benignly referred to as "medical trend"—which trend every year is always upward.

Healthcare costs have risen *every* year since 1960.[1] In just the years 1999–2016, U.S. healthcare spending grew a remarkable 261 percent (see Figure 1).

While many factors contributed—e.g., the aging of the Baby Boomer generation, increasingly advanced (and expensive) medical treatments and technology, and the growth in the number of costly specialty drugs—abusive and arbitrary unchecked price hikes by healthcare providers, especially hospitals, have been a key driver of healthcare inflation. This healthcare inflation is reflected in the dramatic growth in the cost of health insurance, which increased by 213 percent over the same time period (see Figure 2).

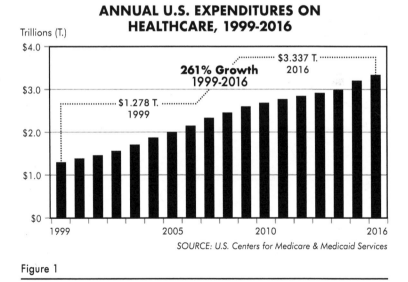

Figure 1

---

[1] "National Health Expenditures Summary Including Share of GDP, CY 1960-2016," Centers for Medicare and Medicaid Services.

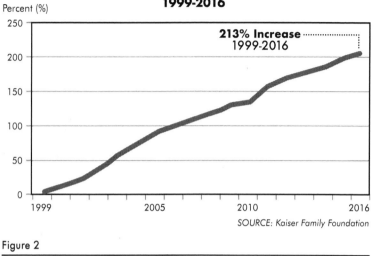

U.S. HEALTH INSURANCE PREMIUMS, 1999-2016

SOURCE: Kaiser Family Foundation

Figure 2

Asleep at the Switch

Healthcare prices are out of control, pricing abuse is rampant, quality can be hit-or-miss, and there is no transparency in healthcare pricing. Yet the BUCAHs seem oblivious . . . and asleep at the switch, allowing the dysfunction of the healthcare Status Quo to continue.

For example, a recent Consumer Reports survey of U.S. pharmacies found that a basket of five popular generic prescription drugs ranged in price from just $66 for all five medications at online mail-order pharmacy Healthwarehouse.com to $928 for the same five drugs at CVS/Target. That's a price change of over 1,300 percent . . . for the exact same drugs (see Figure 3). Yet no BUCAH alerts health plan members to these price differences and guides them to fill their prescriptions at lower-cost pharmacies.

WHICH PHARMACIES HAVE THE BEST RX PRICES?

RETAILER	Pioglitazone (Actos)	Celecoxib (Celebrex)	Duloxetine (Cymbalta)	Atorvastatin (Lipitor)	Clopidogrel (Plavix)	TOTAL PRICE
Health Warehouse.com	$12	$22	$13	$10	$10	$66
Costco [1]	$16	$26	$35	$13	$16	$105
Independents [2]	$19 ($10-$493)	$34 ($11-$295)	$31 ($20-$267)	$15 ($8-$197)	$15 ($8-$260)	$107 ($69-$1,351)
Sam's Club [1]	$20	$38	$31	$20	$45	$153
Walmart	$132	$203	$123	$30	$30	$518
Kmart	$160	$185	$120	$35	$35	$535
Grocery Stores [3]	$113 ($10-$349)	$189 ($46-$250)	$170 ($13-$223)	$32 ($11-$71)	$36 ($7-$224)	$565 ($88-$1,117)
Walgreens	$167	$204	$251	$65	$65	$752
Rite Aid	$255	$194	$170	$128	$119	$866
CVS/Target	$270	$187	$195	$135	$141	$928

1,306% Price Difference

[1] Nonmember prices.

[2] Prices in parentheses are the ranges across sampled stores. Total price reflects the averages of the combined prices for the five drugs at individual independent pharmacies.

[3] Prices in parentheses are the ranges of the averages across sampled stores, including Albertsons, Food Lion, Giant Eagle, H-E-B, Hy-Vee, Kroger, Publix, and others. Total price reflects averages of the combined prices for the five drugs at individual grocery store pharmacies.

SOURCE: Consumer Reports. Shop Around for Lower Drug Prices. April 5, 2018. https://www.consumerreports.org/drug-prices/shop-around-for-better-drug-prices/

Figure 3

Seeing how much CVS charges for drugs, however, it's easy to understand how a pharmacy chain can buy a health insurance company, Aetna, for $69 billion.

Inpatient Surgery

In addition to prescription drugs, the lack of healthcare price transparency and abusive pricing can be seen in hospital quality/cost comparisons that can be found in most any city in the U.S. (see Figure 4).

In New York City, you can have cardiovascular surgery performed at Mount Sinai Hospital, with the highest quality rating, for $64,336. Or you can go 12 miles away to NYU

HOSPITAL PRICING DISPARITIES

Cardiovascular (Heart) Surgery
New York, NY • Hospital Facility Fees Only

Facility	Quality Rating for Procedure	Price	Change
Mount Sinai Hospital	High	$64,336	230%
NYU Hospital Center	Moderately High	$212,707	
Price Difference		$148,371	

Back or Neck Surgery
Dallas, TX • Hospital Facility Fees Only

Facility	Quality Rating for Procedure	Price	Change
UT Southwestern Hospital	High	$20,952	287%
Medical Center of Plano	Moderately High	$81,114	
Price Difference		$60,162	

SOURCE: Surgerate Database (surgerate.com); 2018 Data.

Figure 4

Hospital Center, with a lower quality rating for that procedure, for $212,707. If this information was common knowledge, would anyone choose the lower quality hospital charging 230 percent more for the exact same procedure?

In Dallas, TX, you can choose to have your orthopedic back or neck surgery done at University of Texas Southwestern Hospital, boasting a top-quality rating, for $20,952. Or, less than 19 miles away, you can have your back or neck procedure performed at the Medical Center of Plano, rated lower quality for this procedure, for $81,114. Who, if made aware of the choice, would select a lower-quality facility with the attendant health and infection risks and pay 287 percent more?

These glaring price and quality differentials are common throughout the country. Plus, I haven't mentioned the option of high-quality outpatient surgery centers that bundle all surgical costs—facility fee, surgeon, anesthesia, appliance, etc.—into a single cash price that usually is a fraction of the cost of the same procedure at even the lowest-cost hospital.

Whether it is an inpatient or outpatient procedure, no BUCAH informs plan members of these gross quality and price disparities, leaving every member at risk of choosing a lower-quality, higher-price facility, potentially putting the member's health in greater jeopardy and certainly costing both employee and employer an unnecessary and unwarranted greater expense.

Imaging Tests

Diagnostic imaging testing provides a final example of the extreme pricing disparity and lack of price transparency in healthcare. Not only does the cost for tests such as CT scans and MRIs vary widely from city to city, the cost for one of these diagnostic tests can vary within a city by as much as a factor of 10 or more.

In Tampa, FL, a head/brain CT scan ranges from a low of $224 to a high of $2,804, a more than 1,150 percent swing in price. In Buffalo, NY, the same head/brain CT scan is available for as little as $197, but at a nearby facility can cost as much as $1,105, a 460 percent cost difference. Similarly, you can get a lower-back MRI in Fresno, CA, for $859 or you can travel a couple of miles to pay as much as $4,395 for the exact same test. In Nashville, TN, that same lower-back MRI costs just $453 at one facility but balloons to $2,552 across town (see Figure 5).

Amazingly, massive price variations such as these for imaging and in-patient surgical facilities can be found within a BUCAH

PRICE DISPARITY IN DIAGNOSTIC TESTS

Head/Brain CT Scan Variations in price across and within major U.S. cities			Lower-Back MRI Variations in price across and within major U.S. cities		
City	Price Range	Swing	City	Price Range	Swing
Tampa, FL	$224 - $2,804	1,152%	Fresno, CA	$859 - $4,395	411%
Buffalo, NY	$197 - $1,105	460%	Nashville, TN	$453 - $2,552	463%

SOURCE: Castlight; 2018 Data.

Figure 5

plan provider network, so that both the lowest and highest prices are approved, in-network prices. Other times, paying a cash price to an out-of-network testing facility can be far less expensive than going to an in-network provider. Despite these absurd price disparities, just as with the wide cost differences in pharmacy prices and hospital fees, the BUCAHs provide plan members with no guidance is shopping for diagnostic tests, regardless of the impact on the member's and employer's wallet.

In all these examples, by not directing employees to high-quality/low-cost healthcare, the BUCAHs allow employees seeking healthcare to play Russian Roulette with their employer's money.

Misaligned Incentives

Why have the BUCAHs, multi-billion-dollar organizations with the best talent and resources available, failed to stem the growth of healthcare costs or even address the dysfunctional pricing in the system? It's not that they are *incapable* of reducing the cost of healthcare; they certainly know how to bring down health-care costs. Their spectacular failure points to THE foundational problem in our healthcare system: grossly misaligned incentives.

The health insurance companies lack any financial incentive to reduce healthcare costs and healthcare spending. In fact, the two middlemen in healthcare, the insurance carriers and the insurance brokers, *financially benefit from **rising** healthcare costs.*

Carrier revenue is largely the health insurance premium dollars paid by employers and individual policyholders. Rising healthcare costs force carriers to increase the premiums they charge to reflect the higher cost of goods and services. As medical trend drives premiums higher, the higher premiums boost carrier revenue. A carrier's profit margin on a higher revenue number is . . . more profit.

So the simple financial equation for the BUCAHs and other carriers looks like this:

Positive Medical Trend × Insurance Premiums = Higher Premiums = Increased Carrier Revenue × Carrier Profit Margin = Higher Carrier Income

As healthcare costs have steadily increased, so have the revenue and income of the BUCAHs. In fact, their stock value growth over the past five years has been nothing less than spectacular, *averaging 257 percent growth* (see Figure 6).

FIVE-YEAR BUCAH STOCK VALUE GROWTH & NET REVENUE IN U.S. DOLLAR BILLIONS, AS OF AUGUST 2018

	5-Year Stock Growth	Net Income (August 2018)
Anthem (Blue Cross)	230%	$3.2
UnitedHealthcare	326%	$10.7
Cigna	146%	$2.8
Aetna	315%	$3.6
Humana	269%	$1.5

SOURCE: Morningstar, FactSet, Financial Times. 2018.

Figure 6

The BUCAH's earnings shown in Figure 6 include billions of dollars in higher premiums paid by employers due to increases in healthcare costs that the carriers easily could have prevented. But their financial incentives lead health insurance carriers to *welcome*—not work to avoid—higher healthcare costs.

Likewise, health insurance brokers have misaligned incentives. Brokers usually are paid a commission on the premium dollars for the health insurance they place with employers. When rising healthcare costs push premiums higher, the broker receives an automatic raise. For example, when her employer client receives a 10 percent increase in its health insurance premium at renewal, a broker who is paid commission on the healthcare premium just got a 10 percent increase in her compensation . . . even as her client was being charged more for the same insurance coverage. (Brokers compensated with a per-member-per-month fee instead of commission still have zero financial incentive to do the additional work to control and reduce their client's healthcare costs.)

Furthermore, regardless of whether their compensation is commission or a per-member-per-month fee, the broker is being paid by the insurance company. Since everyone works for whomever signs their paychecks, clearly brokers can't be working for their employer client, no matter how much they claim they are. Unless they are being compensated with fees paid by the employer, brokers work for the carrier. Period.

So both of the middlemen in healthcare—carriers and brokers—have financial incentives that are totally misaligned with the employer that is paying the healthcare bills for its employees.

It should now be easy to understand why healthcare costs continue to increase unabated every year. The C-Suite delegates to the insurance company and their broker responsibility for managing the cost of healthcare, while the carrier and the broker do nothing to lower healthcare costs, turning a blind eye to the dysfunction and abuses in the healthcare system that drive healthcare prices—and their revenue—ever higher.

And it should now be easy to understand why the insurance carriers and their broker partners feel compelled to keep company executives out of the healthcare discussion. The result of the Big Lie is the continued upward trend in the cost of healthcare, by ensuring that employers, as the healthcare payors, never apply to healthcare the purchasing strategies and market discipline they apply to every other aspect of their businesses.

Healthcare's middlemen are best served if employers never attempt to manage the healthcare supply chain and begin to negotiate price and quality with the providers of healthcare.

The Status Quo Wall

The Big Lie has effectively erected a massive, towering wall separating the healthcare payors—employers—on the one side and the healthcare providers—doctors, hospitals, drug companies, etc.—on the other. In the only communication or interaction between these two groups, the providers throw invoices—medical claims—over the wall and the payors throw money—claims payments—back over the wall to the providers.

This metaphorical Status Quo wall is composed, of course, of the carriers and brokers, whose constant repetition of the

Big Lie has convinced almost every CEO and CFO in America to avoid any involvement in the purchase and management of healthcare and to abandon their fiduciary responsibility for their company's now second or third largest expense.

In his Foreword to the Amazon bestseller, *BREAKING THROUGH THE STATUS QUO: How Innovative Companies Are Changing the Benefits Game to Help Their Employees and Boost Their Bottom Line*, GSESP's CFO Bender described his treatment by health insurance brokers:

> *"[S]tatus quo brokers, which is most of them, have treated CFOs and CEOs like mushrooms . . . they've kept us in the dark and fed us a steady diet of manure."*

Benefits Revolution

However, a growing insurrection in employee benefits is challenging the passivity of America's C-Suite in the face of unsustainable healthcare cost increases.

A veritable Benefits Revolution, led by a vanguard of innovative NextGen Benefits Advisers operating across the U.S., is changing the way companies purchase and manage their healthcare.

As Bender describes it, NextGen Benefits Advisers "are working with the CFO to ensure fiduciary oversight, shifting the strategic decision-making on the benefits budget from HR to the C-Suite to engage executive management, and providing supply chain management to the employees' healthcare to promote appropriate utilization of medical services and plan resources."

Having transformed from a Status Quo transactional broker to a consultative adviser, these NextGen Advisers are engaging the C-Suite with strategic financial conversations about the benefits spend. These advisers are eschewing commission compensation in favor of employer-paid fees, which provide transparency.

But even more important than the compensation transparency of fees, they then are putting part of their fee *at risk to guarantee bottom-line results* . . . specifically real, year-over-year reductions in the cost of healthcare. This is the most essential innovation of the Benefits Revolution, aligning the adviser's incentives with the employer client.

The 2017 Employee Benefit Adviser of the Year, Mick Rodgers of Boston's Axial Benefits Group, explains in *BREAKING THROUGH THE STATUS QUO* why performance-based fees are such an important development in employee benefits:

> *"In the new fee-for-performance employee benefits purchasing structure, advisers are paid more when an employer's benefits program performs better. Not only does this help build trust, it also motivates advisers to continually improve program options and seek new ways to optimize performance."*

By putting their fees at risk, NextGen Advisers are moving their chair around the table to sit next to the employer, unheard of in employee benefits. This alignment incentivizes the adviser to do the hard work necessary to improve the benefits and lower the employer's healthcare costs. While the move to performance-based fees is essential, a new role for the benefits adviser is the most important change in how employee benefits are bought in the NextGen Benefits model.

Supply Chain Management

In the most high-impact innovation of the Benefits Revolution and the reason they can guarantee cost savings, NextGen Benefits Advisers are taking on the role of manager of the healthcare supply chain to improve medical outcomes and enhance employee benefits while controlling and lowering healthcare costs.

Again, CFO Bender: "[T]he real problem with employee benefits is that we in the C-Suite simply have not treated our benefits like we do every other key part of our business. . . . Supply chain management? Of course, for every single business unit in the company . . . except benefits. . . . And, just as I don't personally do supply chain management for my other business units, I don't have to with benefits. That's what my NextGen Benefits Adviser does."

Unlike the easily disintermediated broker middleman, the NextGen Benefits Adviser plays an integral role in the benefits process. As both financial strategist and manager of the Healthcare Value Chain, the adviser contributes to both the operational and financial goals of the company and provides the valuable alternative to the Status Quo broker that is needed to begin fixing healthcare.

But, first, before employers and their NextGen Benefits Advisers can begin to manage the healthcare supply chain, employers have to take back control of their health plan from the BUCAHs.

Disintermediate the Middlemen

Disintermediation of any long-serving intermediary should not be done arbitrarily and without due consideration. A supply chain management best practice is a three-step exercise to evaluate whether or not disintermediation would be advantageous. After analyzing if the intermediary supports a company's Financial and Operational objectives, the process then considers and compares available Alternatives to the intermediary.

When applied to health insurance companies including the BUCAHs, this disintermediation exercise quickly leads to the unavoidable conclusion that disintermediation of the BUCAHs would be a tremendous benefit to the healthcare supply chain.

While the financial implications of disintermediation are profound, the operational considerations are much more to the point, since it's not possible for the NextGen Benefits Adviser to manage the supply chain as long as a BUCAH is running the employer's health plan.

Once the BUCAH is disintermediated, the employer and its adviser have unfettered access to claims data for predictive analytics and can implement any number of highly effective cost-containment and supply chain management strategies.

Managing the Healthcare Value Chain

With control of the health plan, NextGen Benefits Advisers employ supply chain management techniques to manage and improve the Healthcare Value Chain. Value chain is defined as a process that enhances the value of a good or service to provide a superior outcome. In the case of healthcare, managing the value chain is ensuring that "the right patients are getting the right care, at the right time, in the right place, at the right price," as formulated by Deborah L. Ault, RN, MBA, president of Ault International Medical Management, a leading provider of medical management services.

Healthcare Value Chain management employs strategies and techniques including medical management, data mining and predictive analytics, reference-based pricing or reimbursement, direct contracting with healthcare providers, domestic and international medical travel, telemedicine, bundled-price surgery centers, Direct Primary Care, expert medical opinion, cost-transparency tools, fiduciary pharmacy benefit management, specialty drug cost-mitigation, and population health management.

As the Benefits Revolution grows and expands, NextGen Benefits Advisers are discovering—and the market is developing—new strategies and tools to improve healthcare outcomes and lower the cost of healthcare.

NextGen Benefits Case Studies

NextGen Benefits Advisers (NextGen Advisers) are producing bottom-line results for employers across the U.S. by managing the Healthcare Value Chain. In the case studies below, all are disintermediating the health insurance company and moving the client to an alternative funding strategy that allows full control of the benefits plan and budget. While the specific strategies vary, all are implementing NextGen supply chain management strategies to manage the Value Chain. Just these few real-world case studies prove that the strategies work in any market with any size group and produce remarkable results: better benefits for the employees at a much lower cost for the employers.

- **39% YEAR-OVER-YEAR SAVINGS**: In Massachusetts, the CEO of **ProMedical** (65 employees) engaged Benefit Adviser of the Year Mick Rodgers of Axial Benefits Group to manage the benefits spend. Putting the firm into a Healthcare Purchasing Coalition and introducing supply chain management strategies, Rodgers reduced ProMedical's year-over-year benefits spend by 39 percent in just one year, saving the company $363,773. And while Rodgers was lowering the cost of healthcare, in year one he also reduced the employees' deductible by $500.

- **$1.03 MILLION IN SAVINGS:** In California, NextGen Adviser Craig Lack of ENERGI was retained by a large **School District Joint Powers Authority** (JPA) to reduce their benefits spend. Using just a single NextGen Benefits strategy, by the end of 12 months the JPA had saved over $1 million in plan costs while saving employees hundreds of thousands of dollars in out-of-pocket expenses.

- **37% YEAR-OVER-YEAR SAVINGS:** In Indiana, NextGen Adviser Jeff Fox of H.J. Spier implemented a key NextGen strategy in 2017 with **Washington Township** in Hendricks County (61 employees), which had a per-employee-per-year (PEPY) healthcare spend of $21,230. Jeff moved the Township to a direct contract with healthcare provider Hendricks Regional Health (HRH), which, in addition to lower healthcare costs, provided the Township employees with access to near-site clinics and a concierge service to help them navigate the healthcare system. After a year, the HRH Network helped reduce the Township's PEPY to just $13,328, a 37.2 percent drop that allowed the Township to accumulate a reserve fund with over $500,000 in unused claims dollars.

- **$1.3 MILLION IN RX SAVINGS:** In Georgia, the Board of Commissioners of **Cherokee County, GA** (1,300 employees) brought in NextGen Adviser Spencer Allen of IOA in Atlanta to address their out-of-control drug spend. Using NextGen cost-containment strategies, at the end of 2017 Allen had reduced the total prescription drug spend by 38 percent, saving the county $1.3 million.

- **45% YEAR-OVER-YEAR SAVINGS:** In Montana, the owner of **Ace Hardware Great Falls** (32 employees) engaged NextGen Adviser Dawn Sheue of Summit Insurance Services to manage the company's benefits spend. Moving the company from a fully-insured to a level-funded health plan with NextGen cost-containment strategies, after just the first 12 months Sheue had reduced the company's year-over-year benefits spend by over 45 percent, without increasing the deductible or co-insurance. And because in this funding arrangement any claims dollars that don't get spent go to the employer instead of the insurance company, Sheue presented the owner with a $45,621 refund check for unused claims dollars.

- **36% YEAR-OVER-YEAR SAVINGS:** In New Jersey, the CEO of **New Jersey Door Works** (52 employees) hired John Sbrocco, Gary Bender's NextGen Benefits Adviser, in 2016 to manage their benefits spend. Implementing an alternative funding strategy, Sbrocco then deployed several NextGen cost-containment strategies that, by the end of year one, reduced the healthcare spend by 36 percent, saving the company over $200,000 over the previous year without any new cost-shifting to employees. By the end of 2017, Sbrocco reduced the annual spend by an additional two percent and presented the CEO with a refund check for $162,250 in unused claims dollars.

Advancing the Revolution

The Benefits Revolution is waking up the C-Suite to the Big Lie of the BUCAHs and their broker agents that executives are powerless in the face of increasing healthcare costs. As the revolution spreads and disrupts the Status Quo, CEOs and CFOs across the country are engaging and changing the way they purchase and manage their healthcare.

Partnering with NextGen Benefits Advisers whose incentives are aligned with their own, employers are seizing control of their benefits spend by disintermediating the BUCAH and broker middlemen.

Working closely with the C-Suite on financial strategy around the benefits spend, NextGen Advisers are managing the Healthcare Value Chain on behalf of the CEO and CFO. As their supply chain strategies take effect, medical outcomes are improving for employees and the cost of healthcare is coming down, making healthcare affordable again for both employees and employers.

As NextGen Benefits Advisers debunk healthcare's Big Lie across the country, as more and more employers join the Benefits Revolution, more and more C-Suites are taking control of their healthcare spend to make healthcare affordable again. *Vive la revolution!*

NELSON L. GRISWOLD

Chairman
Association for Insurance Leadership
Nashville, TN

Nelson Griswold is recognized as one the industry's leading authorities on how the changes brought by the ACA are creating an unprecedented opportunity for employers finally to take control of their benefits spend while improving both their benefits and the healthcare outcomes for their employees. He is co-author of the book, *Doing More with Less: Innovative Strategies for HR*, a handbook for HR and benefits professionals.

One of the premier thought leaders in the benefits industry, Nelson also is the author of the industry bestseller, *DO OR DIE: Reinventing Your Benefits Agency for Post-Reform Success*, a blueprint for agency leaders to re-engineer their firm to align their interests to match their clients' interests, bring innovative business solutions, and drive actual results. A respected consultant to employee benefits firms across the country, his clients include Aon Hewitt, HUB, and top independent agencies.

He is a leading strategic consultant on employee engagement and next-generation enrollment strategies to insurance companies including Aetna, Trustmark, Aflac, Humana, Allstate, Principal Financial, Anthem, RBC Insurance of Canada, and Assurant. He also advises a number of companies using technology and other innovative strategies to change and improve the benefits landscape.

A monthly columnist for *Employee Benefit Adviser* magazine, Nelson also writes for *Employee Benefit News*, *BenefitsPro*, *HealthCare Consumerism Solutions*, and other leading industry publications. An in-demand keynote speaker and presenter at industry conferences, he serves on the boards of the Voluntary Benefits Association and the Workplace Benefits Association.

www.AIL-assn.org
nelson@insurancebottomline.com
615.369.0618

CHAPTER **TWO**

Realigning Incentives

*How to Turn Your Benefits Plan
Into a Strategic Advantage*

JIM BLACHEK

A s a business leader, you likely grapple with maximizing your budget, recruiting and retaining talented employees, and strengthening your competitive advantages. What many leaders don't know, however, is that their benefits plan can improve all three of those areas.

Your benefits plan is a hidden source of growth for your business, but the traditional benefits broker approach is unlikely to unlock its full potential. The broker model does not account for the full scope of your business goals when developing your business plan. They have an off-the-shelf product and try to fit all of their customers into that box. A true adviser takes a different approach with your benefits: they work with you to build a plan that helps your business grow.

Your adviser can create a new strategic advantage for your business by developing a plan that:

- Aligns with all stakeholders' goals and incentives
- Evolves with your business to support key goals
- Puts your employees first

By working with an adviser who strives to use your benefits plan to grow your company, your plan will stop being an ever-increasing annual expense. Instead, you'll have a tool that you can use to redistribute savings and to boost employee health and morale.

Here's how you can start to use all the opportunities your benefits plan has to offer:

Work With an Adviser Whose Incentives Match Yours

Standard brokers work on a commission-based model, which means that their focus is on selling you the plan that will get them paid the most, collecting their paycheck, and then disappearing until it's time to renegotiate your plan the following year. The only guarantee you have about the cost of your plan is that it's going to keep rising (as much as 6 percent this year alone, according to an Aon healthcare survey), and your broker isn't going to strike any deals with you that will put their own paycheck at risk.

An adviser who's worthwhile will help build a plan that gets all stakeholders working toward the same ultimate goal. The right benefits plan will satisfy:

- You
- Your employees
- Your third-party administrator/your insurer
- Your pharmacy benefits manager
- Your adviser

Advisers get paid based on how much they can help you. For example, partner with a firm that offers a performance guarantee, which promises that if the results of our services don't align with what they discussed with you, they don't make a profit. If your broker isn't willing to make promises that would put their own pay at risk if they don't deliver are likely not working toward the same goal as you are.

Working with an adviser whose incentives align with yours makes the benefits negotiation process not only more pleasant, but also more efficient. Your business will reap the profits of having an adviser who wants the same things you do—namely, a plan that maximizes employee benefits without blowing through your budget. Your adviser will also strategize with your top-level employees so that the money you save on your premiums goes to where it can help the most, working with your C-suite to find savings throughout your benefits plan and putting the funds where they are needed most.

Creating a plan that gives everyone involved what they're looking for is the best way to know that your adviser is truly working *for* you. Like every other aspect of your business, your benefits plan will be more effective when everyone it affects is happy with the costs and results associated with it, and that starts by working with an adviser who wants the same results as you do.

Develop a Plan That Evolves With Your Business

Think of your benefits plan as a train and your adviser as the conductor: the train may have a predetermined track that will take it to its destination (you have to have a benefits plan), but if the destination changes, it's up to the conductor to make any necessary changes and communicate with the right people so that the cargo still gets where it needs to go.

You, your business leaders, and your adviser should be sitting down throughout the year and discussing the performance of your benefits plan, making adjustments and planning for a higher-performing future. If there are any changes that could be made to help increase your savings, your adviser should be working to evolve your plan to fit your needs rather than convincing you to purchase a one-size-fits-all plan. Otherwise, you're going to end up either paying too much for lower-quality benefits, or your employees won't get the healthcare they need.

Work With Insurers Who Have a Fiduciary Responsibility to You and Your Employees

Did you know that if you are currently using a BUCA (Blue Cross, United HealthCare, Cigna, Aetna) or other major insurer that they have a disincentive to keep your plan costs low? The ACA requires all health insurers to spend, on average, a minimum of 80 percent of every premium dollar on claim related costs. This only leaves the insurer with 20 cents on the dollar for potential profit. The insurers are beholden to their stockholders to increase profits and since the passage of ACA law in 2010 their share prices have climbed dramatically.

For the carrier to increase their profits they have been increasing plan costs at a tremendous rate. One of the ways the carriers are profiting is the relationships they have with the major

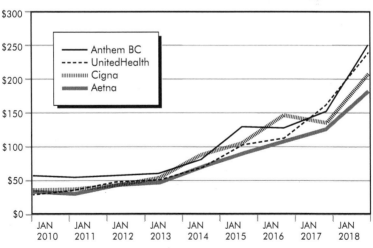

SHARE PRICES OVER TIME FROM THE LARGEST HEALTH INSURANCE COMPANIES

SOURCE: "Stock Summary." Stock Profile. Ameritrade.com. Accessed September 18, 2018.
https://research.tdameritrade.com/grid/public/research/stocks/summary.

pharmacy benefit managers (PBM). The PBMs are also not fiduciarily responsible to the plan holder but to their stockholders. Studies have shown that up to 50 percent of the prescription cost is unnecessary and with the correct PBM partners can be eliminated and those savings passed on directly to the plan holder.

Work with an advisor who will create a transparent unbundled self-funded plan that eliminates the carrier profits and PBM overcharges and allows the plan holder (employer) to keep those profits.

Prioritize Your Employees

Your benefits plan is a powerful recruiting and retention tool, and your business will thrive if you construct your plan with an employee focus. Workers consistently and overwhelmingly name benefits plan as one of their key considerations when choosing an employer, and if your business can offer them a high-quality healthcare plan, you're going to give yourself a competitive advantage even against larger companies when it comes to attracting and keeping top talent.

Here's what focusing your plan on your employees' interests can do:

- **Create savings from the top down.** Developing a plan that's personalized not only for your business, but also your individual workers might sound like it would be more expensive, but the reality is that it can save you money. For example, an advisor can help you develop a

level or gap-funded plan that focuses on your employees' specific needs rather than assuming that every staff
member will have to use the most expensive aspects of
your benefits plan. This ensures that high-risk employees
can get guaranteed coverage while keeping out-of-pocket
costs low for employees who generally don't require
anything beyond maintenance or prevention-based
healthcare.

- **Develop more convenient solutions for your employees.** Working with an adviser who looks for innovative
solutions can benefit your employees while cutting costs
for you. By purchasing a plan that includes telemedicine, your employees don't have to be inconvenienced
by driving to and from the doctor's office and sitting in
the waiting room. You, in turn, save money by making this change to your plan and now have additional
funds to spend elsewhere in your business. At its roots,
an adjustment like this is benefitting your employees,
but its effects can be felt throughout other areas of the
company as well.

- **Create a health plan that rewards employees for being
better healthcare consumers.** Work with an advisor
who can design a plan that rewards employees/members
who use high quality providers while accessing the most
cost-effective ones, creating a high value outcome. The
employee/member wins by receiving higher quality care,

a zero out-of-pocket plan option for using the High Value provider, and the plan wins by incentivizing the employee/member to use the high value provider who has a much more cost effective option than would otherwise have occurred, saving the plan thousands of dollars.

- **Limit resources spent on recruiting and training.** The time and expenses associated with bringing on new employees are also decreased by developing a plan that puts your workers first. The savings associated with hiring new talent can be redistributed elsewhere in your business when your existing employees don't feel like they have to look at other employment options for better healthcare. A better plan will also encourage your more skilled employees to continue working for you, and better talent might be drawn to your company if you can offer them better benefits than your competition.

- **Ultimately you win when your employees win.** All plan dollars are driven by what healthcare experiences the members choose. If you provide them with the tools and strategies to improve their healthcare experience, then you, the employer, will begin to reduce your costs allowing you to begin to truly control your cost of healthcare while at the same time improving the benefits offered to your members.

Unlock Your Plan's Full Potential

Your benefits plan is a powerful tool, and if you treat it as just another business expense, you run the risk of overspending, losing valuable employees, and falling behind your competition. Working with an adaptable adviser who has aligned incentives and can keep your employees happy is the best way to turn your plan into a strategic opportunity to help your business thrive in a competitive market. Before you settle for a benefits plan that drains your budget and frustrates your employees, talk with an adviser who has aligned with you who wants to see your business grow just as much as you do.

JAMES "JIM" BLACHEK

Principal and Co-founder
The Benefits Group, LLC
Clarks Summit, PA

Jim Blachek began his career in the late 80s as a traditional life and investment agent with Equitable of NY. Blachek is co-founder and principal of The Benefits Group, LLC, a boutique *NextGen Benefits Firm* based in Northeastern Pennsylvania. The Benefits Group, LLC was founded on the principal of helping employers navigate the healthcare landscape. Blachek firmly believes in embracing a consultative strategic process to effectively reduce the cost of healthcare. Working with over 400 corporate clients encompassing tens of thousands of employees he has become their partner in that quest.

Blachek embraces a fundamental mission and passion of an employee centric approach to managing the cost of healthcare. All strategies and tools are focused on assisting an employee to have greater access to higher quality healthcare all while driving down employer and employee cost. No tool or strategy will be successful without proper employee engagement and education. They are the key to driving down cost. Blachek has published numerous articles on this topic.

Blachek, along with co-founder Jeff Haudenschield, is a proud member and advisor of *NextGen Benefits Mastermind Partners*, a national partnership of like minded advisers who are determined to change the face of healthcare and "Break the Status Quo" to take control of their cost of healthcare.

www.benegroup.net
jim@benegroup.net
570.351.1158

CHAPTER **THREE**

Healthcare Costs Are Killing Your Competitiveness and What to Do About It

ROBERT SLAYTON

Healthcare expenses are typically the second or third largest spend an organization makes after employee salaries. If not managed well, they can make you fall behind your competitors. This chapter focuses on both the problem and several solutions to help companies be the best and most profitable in their industry.

The Problem — Real Employee Compensation Is Flat to Negative

Your annual salary increase to employees is getting eaten up by increased deductibles, premiums, and spending. According to

**COMPENSATION, INCLUDING BENEFITS,
VERSUS TAKE-HOME PAY**

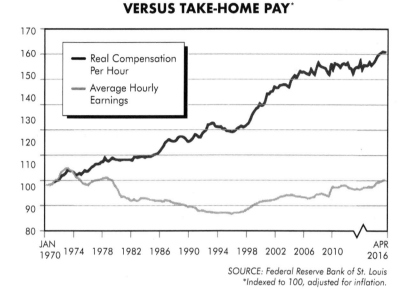

SOURCE: Federal Reserve Bank of St. Louis
*Indexed to 100, adjusted for inflation.

a RAND Corporation study,[1] over the last 10 years, 79 percent of an employee's salary increase is eaten up by these things. A follow up two years later (12 years total) showed that middle class families only had an extra $51/month more in their paycheck to help pay for things such as food, clothing, and utilities. This means that over time, employees are WORSE off after the increase than before. This leads to stressed employees who may be looking for a better deal at a competitor.

Fifty percent of the musculoskeletal treatments you are paying for are ineffective; 4.5 percent of our national GDP

---

[1] Kellermann, D. I. (2011). *How Does Growth in Health Care Costs Affect the American Family?* Santa Monica: RAND Corporation. Retrieved from https://www.rand.org/pubs/research_briefs/RB9605.html

is taken up by musculoskeletal disorders. Furthermore, the leading cause of disability in the United States is due to these disorders.[2] The U.S. performs twice the number of treatments as all of the other industrialized nations with NO BETTER OUTCOMES. By extrapolation, one-half of the musculoskeletal treatments your employees are going through are not going to have a positive outcome.[2]

In addition, two-thirds of all cancer drugs released have NO EVIDENCE that they work.[3]

CANCER DRUG EFFECTIVENESS

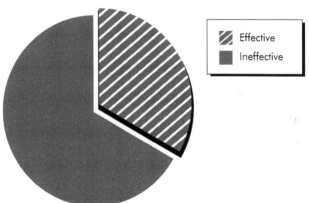

SOURCE: Bone and Joint Initiative USA. (2014). The Big Picture: The Burden of Musculoskeletal Disease in the United States. http://www.boneandjointburden.org/2014-report/i0/big-picture

[2] Bone and Joint Initiative USA. (2014). The Big Picture: The Burden of Musculoskeletal Disease in the United States. Retrieved from http://www.boneandjointburden.org/2014-report/i0/big-picture

[3] Vinay Prasad, M. M. (2015). Cancer Drugs Approved on the Basis of a Surrogate End Point and Subsequent Overall Survival. *JAMA Internal Medicine.* doi:doi:10.1001/jamainternmed.2015.5868

You Are Paying For Incorrect Diagnoses

Twenty-eight percent of all cancers are misdiagnosed.[4] People are being treated for something they either don't have or are treated for the wrong kind of cancer. The treatment won't work which means that you continue to pay as they escalate the measures taken to save the person's life.

According to a 2017 study,[5] 88 percent of patients who visited the Mayo Clinic for a second opinion on a complex procedure go home with a new or refined diagnosis, changing their care plan and potentially saving their lives.

Most Insurance Brokers Benefit When Your Rates/ Costs Go Up

Status quo brokers are not incented to help you manage costs as they typically make more money when your costs go up. Many times brokers receive a percentage of the commissions and also bonuses for keeping the business with an insurance company, even though it isn't in the best interest of the employer.

Insurance Companies Benefit When Costs Go Up

Due to the Affordable Care Act's Medical Loss Ratio, insurance companies are incented to accept HIGHER costs from medical providers. Insurance companies are required to pay out 85 percent

---

[4] Ducharme, J. (2013, January 31). Misdiagnosing Cancer is More Common Than We Think. *Boston Wellness*. Retrieved from http://www.bostonmagazine. com/health/blog/2013/01/31study-cancer-misdiagnose/
[5] Monica Van Such, R. L. (2017, April 4). Extent of diagnositc agreement among medical referrals. *Journal of Evaluation in Clinical Practice, Volume 23, Issue 4*.

of every dollar of premium in the form of a patient benefit. This means that if the cost of a procedure is twice as much this year as the prior year, then they can raise the premium and keep twice as much money. For example, if a procedure costs $10,000, then the insurance company can charge $11,764 (85% of $11,764 = $10,000). The insurance company keeps $1,764. If that same procedure costs $20,000, then the insurance company can charge $23,529 in premium and keep $3,529.

Selling Internationally?

If you sell internationally, you are at a nine percent COST DIS-ADVANTAGE as compared to countries such as Germany, Korea, and Australia, as a result of our higher healthcare spending.[6]

The Bottom Line

You are paying for misdiagnoses, treatments that don't work, and prescriptions that aren't effective. In addition, the majority of healthcare costs typically come from a small percentage of people who rack up huge claims. Manage this population well and you become more competitive.

Current "status quo brokers," including larger brokers, have a disincentive to help you minimize the cost of healthcare and insurance. Many also lack a fundamental understanding of the healthcare industry. This means they can't help you reduce your

---

[6] Chase, D. (2017). *The CEO's Guide To Restoring The American Dream.* Seattle: Health Rosetta Media.

costs while at the same time help employees and their families manage major health events.

The Solution

Here are several of the most successful strategies to help you, the employer, reduce your medical spending while increasing the certainty of that spend (minimizing the variability of that spend). As a bonus, these solutions increase the quality of care for your employees and their families.

If you implement these strategies, you may be able to save an employee or family member's life.

Success Strategy 1: Find the Right NextGeneration Benefits Adviser

Ask your broker what they are doing TODAY to reduce the frequency and severity of claims. If there aren't specific programs with measurable results, then you need another broker. Ask your broker what additional measures are in your plan to cut your surgical and pharmaceutical spend. Hint: saying that the insurance carrier or TPA handles those items is NOT a valid answer.

If your broker's income is not tied to reducing costs and minimizing your insurance renewal, then chances are they make more money with increased premiums. This is a conflict of interest with the employer and CFO. If you work with a large broker, they usually make extra money in the form of bonuses that they are NOT disclosing to you. You may believe that they are required to disclose all compensation on the Form 5500 (for groups with 100 or more people enrolled), but this is incorrect.

Bonuses to brokers are not broken out by company so need not be included in their compensation on the 5500.

Furthermore, if you don't incent your broker to decrease costs (thereby raising earnings) and increase the quality of the plan, then nothing will change and you'll be stuck with the same excuses as the prior year for the reason why health insurance costs keep going up.

Success Strategy 2: Second Guess the Medical Establishment by Making Second Opinions Mandatory and Using an Independent Medical Management Company (MMC)

Would you like to save a life? Would you like to sleep at night with a warm fuzzy feeling that you are doing more to help your employees and their families than any other company in your industry?

The first step is to make second opinions on major diagnoses mandatory. Any treatment that needs prior authorization can fall into this category. You can put the onus on the employee to get this opinion, but our recommendation is to use a company that specializes in this. The reason is you want the second opinion to come from a top medical professional in the industry for that problem or issue. You could also make an independent agreement with a place such as the Mayo Clinic in order to do the review.

Generally, this second opinion involves sending the tests and notes from the existing doctor to the specialist for the review. If the specialist agrees, then an effective treatment plan can be developed for the condition. Remember the statistic quoted above about 88 percent of all complex diagnoses being not detailed enough to form an effective treatment plan? That's how you change this.

The second, and equally important, step is to engage an independent medical management company (MMC). If you can integrate them into your medical plan so the employee or family member must talk to them before proceeding with treatment, the better. If it is integrated with your TPA or insurance carrier (meaning that they share information with the MMC), then the MMC can proactively reach out to the impacted member to work with them.

The problem with the way our medical community works today is when a person is diagnosed with a major condition, the primary care doctor recommends a specialist who is typically within the same practice. The impacted member sees the specialist, has more tests, is diagnosed and told what they need to do and who will be doing the treatment (or surgery). This is without regard to the actual quality of the diagnosis/specialist/surgeon.

What needs to happen is a frank discussion about the diagnosis and suggested treatment plan with someone who has DATA.

The representative from the MMC (typically a nurse) will talk to the person about their diagnosis and potential outcomes based upon treatment plans. For example, the nurse may say that 85 out of 100 people who get X procedure done are alive after five years. But if you do Y procedure, 98 out of 100 people are alive after five years. If the person thinks this other treatment plan may be better, then the nurse suggests they go back to their doctor and have a discussion about it.

Assuming the person needs something like surgery, the MMC has all of the quality and cost data for EVERY medical professional in the United States and knows how to interpret it. They will help find the BEST person to do the treatment, surgery or procedure. Typically, the doctor who does the most procedures in a month has the best outcomes and almost every time, is the lowest cost. Instead of relying on friends, family, and doctors about subjective experiences with surgeons, you actually get the best doctors available.

The medical management company will also help the person properly prepare for the procedure and talk to the person after surgery to assure they are adhering to their treatment plan.

Success Strategy 3: Use a Responsible and Fair Pharmacy Benefit Manager (PBM)

Your PBM should provide a 100 percent passthrough pricing (you pay a flat per-member, per-month flat fee and receive back any rebates due) and has the ability to source drugs from other countries.

The biggest black box in the medical industry is the pharmacy industry. Drug companies are raising prices on drugs that have been out in the market for twenty years. Producing "me too" drugs—drugs that treat the same condition as several other drugs. Only developing "blockbuster" drugs that they can charge up to $1 million a year to treat a condition.

The PBM's job is to buy drugs in bulk and thereby receive discounts on those drugs for the employer/employee. If you read the contracts the typical PBM uses, they are biased toward their profit at the expense of the employer. Usually manufacturer rebates are not mentioned which means the PBM can make more profit on the backs of the corporations that employ them (the PBM keeps the rebates and does not pass them along to the employer).

Using a PBM that charges a per member per month flat fee or some similar arrangement is advantageous as there is no incentive for them to choose the higher "average price" on the day the script was filled than the lower "average price." By the way, yes, there are multiple prices on the same day for the same drug. The PBM can choose which price to use.

I like to employ a PBM that has the ability to either source drugs from a foreign country (e.g. Canada) or at least allow for another company to source those drugs for the employee. Sometimes the savings are dramatic (paying $900 instead of $4,000).

Finally, a PBM or MMC can work with employees about their drug selections when they require a specialty drug. An employee may qualify for a manufacturer coupon which means they pay little to nothing for a very expensive drug. This means the employer doesn't pay for the drug either.

Success Strategy 4: Take a Portion of Your Savings and Enhance the Employees' Benefits

This single strategy will save you money over time and reduce turn over. When you are saving at least $1,000 per employee per year (usually more), it makes sense to reinvest some of that savings back into your employees. Ideas include lowering their deductibles, paying for chronic medications, introducing telemedicine, and putting in place enhanced benefits. A dollar spent in enriching benefits is a much better deal than giving a dollar raise.

Think of it this way. When you give a person a $1.00 per hour raise, the true cost to the company, taking into account FICA, 401(k), and other employer contributions, is usually around $1.20. If you take the same $1.00 and enhance their benefit, then the company gets a full $1.00 deduction along with creating an ROI.

Success Strategy 5: Immediately Reduce Your Medical Spending 5% Without Changing Anything

If you are a self-insured health plan, then you typically have an individual stop loss above of $100,000 (typically $200,000+). What if you could arbitrage this stop loss down to $8,000 or less while giving the unhealthiest people an incentive to move off of your medical plan? Would you be interested?

This process has been around and successfully implemented for over seventeen years. It's available for you to take advantage of now.

You set up a program where you give a spouse who has access to another group health insurance plan money to pay for their deductible and coinsurance for that other plan if they move to that other plan. Furthermore, if your employee moves to that other plan, you do the same for them.

The unhealthiest people are the ones who burn through the deductible and out-of-pocket maximums every year, so they love the idea of someone else paying for it for them.

One of the common questions I receive is, "What if everyone took this deal?" My response is that if a healthy person takes the deal, that's great because you only pay IF the person has a claim. Therefore, a healthy person wouldn't use the program or would use very little of the money set aside, AND you save your cost of insuring them.

Final Thoughts

If you understand how the healthcare marketplace works, its strengths and weaknesses, then you can put a plan in place to capitalize on it to reduce your costs while at the same time giving your employees a better experience with their benefits package. This leads to reduced turnover and higher employee satisfaction along with your ability to use the freed-up funds to reinvest in your company or compete more competitively in the marketplace.

ROBERT SLAYTON

President
Robert Slayton & Associates, Inc.
Naperville, IL

Robert has been in the industry for over 15 years and specializes in helping employers manage the healthcare supply chain to create superior employee outcomes while freeing up money to be used to expand an organization's mission.

He is an expert on health insurance and has been quoted in trade magazines and the popular press (such as Crains, Chicago Tribune, U.S. News & World Report, MSNBC.com, FoxNews, The Washington Examiner, and Yahoo Hotjobs).

Every year, employers see their investment in employee healthcare increase. Most executives feel helpless and are unable to reign in those costs which now represent their number two or number three budget line item.

Historically, it was nearly impossible to predict and control a company's healthcare budget, but today, due to new solutions, strategies, technology, and a wealth of data, business leaders can (and are) taking back control of their healthcare budgets to reclaim trapped profits while actually creating healthier, happier employees that are more fulfilled and more productive.

As a next generation benefits adviser, Robert has the privilege of helping employers achieve those game—changing results and break through the status quo of just accepting increasing healthcare costs year after year.

Brokering insurance and negotiating the lowest cost increase is no longer a sustainable, viable, or preferred approach to managing a company's healthcare investment. What's required today is a legitimate consultative and strategic approach solves the problem long-term.

This new approach is healthcare supply chain management. This model allows companies to apply the same effective cost-control practices they leverage in other parts of the organization to their healthcare costs—the process eliminates wasted expenses, redirects dollars to produce a measurable ROI, and optimizes the employee healthcare experience creating a more loyal, productive, and profitable workforce.

If you want happier and more productive employees, and a long-term healthcare strategy that expands your mission, then let's chat. It is not certain that his approach will work for your organization, but he's willing to invest a few minutes to find out and answer your questions.

Robert is Past President of the Illinois State Association of Health Underwriters (ISAHU) and Past Legislative Co-Chair for the DuPage Association of Health Underwriters (DAHU).

He holds a Master's of Science Degree in Education in Counseling from Northern Illinois University and a Bachelor's Degree in Psychology from the University of Michigan (with a minor in International Business).

Robert and his wife Susan live in Naperville, Illinois, with their two children. He enjoys spending time with his family (and dog), reading, and being active in his community. His most recent position is as Chairman of the Permanent Funds Committee at his church. Want to talk about your specific situation? Schedule an appointment with Robert here: www.slaytonins.com/30-min

www.slaytonins.com
robert@slaytonins.com
630.779.1144

CHAPTER FOUR

Maximizing Your Healthcare Supply Chain

BRIAN TSCHETTER

A Little History

When I was a new Vice President at Bank of America Credit Card my first assignment was to fix the decline of existing accounts and the spiral of card balances. I found myself presenting the findings and recommendations to the Vice Chairman of the Consumer Division. The Credit Card Division had lost $900 million in balances in less than 12 months; which was almost 10% annualized decrease to a $11 billion division. The numbers painted an obvious picture that the status quo was not working and was not accepted by customers. I had recently finished a similar challenge at Mellon Bank, a smaller bank with the same challenges.

My surprise was arguing the findings with the Vice Chairman. He ran the credit card division back when it was BankAmericard, the beginning of VISA bank card association. This was hallowed ground, where bank cards started. Surely he would understand the key metrics, the obvious changes. So we discussed and debated. He reluctantly conceded we needed to move away from the status quo; but only after we all understood the same cost drivers. Status quo thinking was challenged by results, by consumer changes. We could either plan and adopt or accept decline. We moved forward but had to realize the status quo was not working and change our strategy, change our tactics. The status quo no longer worked.

I discovered that no one wanted to risk their executive job or reputation by not following the status quo. That's why it got kicked up to the Vice Chairman for approval, that's why they had a lowly Vice President present the findings, recommendation, and argument. Real change from the status quo needs commitment from the top of the organization and must be endorsed from the top.

The scenario around employer medical plans has similar status quo characteristics. The cost and cost increases appear unsustainable for employers and employees. The premiums have become a significant portion of employee compensation and its impacting the bottom line. The most difficult step may be realizing the status quo is no longer acceptable. No one moves from the status quo unless it's necessary, but for many employers it is now necessary. However, to make a change from the status quo, the commitment, endorsement, and understanding must come from the top of the organization.

Healthcare Supply Chain

When the status quo is no longer affordable, or employers have had enough, they will need to break down the healthcare supply chain, then focus on the issues to improve their cost and quality. The solutions are in managing the Healthcare Value Chain. That's not different than any other company expense. The good news is that there are many new strategies and tactics that improve employee healthcare, employee experience, and contain the cost. The best strategy is determined by the employer because every employer has a unique situation.

Before implementing the cost containment and quality measure, be sure to include the employees in the strategy and objectives. As with any significant change, employees will need multiple communications and objectives continually reinforced by the top of the company.

Fully-Insured

Fully-insured carrier plans have their own bundled healthcare supply chain. It's a convenient package with customer service, provider networks, care management, case management, and pharmacy. All professionally bundled with years of continuity and large networks of providers. All you need to do is pay the premium.

When you try to find the key cost drivers, little if any reporting is available to the employer. You may get some reporting for employers with 100-plus employees, a bit more with 300-plus employees. But if you have less than 100 employees, you're likely not to get any official reporting. Just a few notes from the underwriter and talk about trends, pools etc. How can you understand the challenge without any reporting? You're limited to competitively shopping one fully-insured with the other fully-insured carriers with the hope you'll find one with a pricing anomaly to your advantage. There's not much else you can do, and that's what perpetuates the status quo. Rate increases with poorer employee plans.

They have improved their methods, processes, and continue to improve, but with fully-insured plans everything is bundled with their objectives in mind. Good, bad, or indifferent, their choices are your choices. Their process is your process, you have no real options or choices. The problem is: their objectives are not necessarily the employers. For example, they process a lot of claims. Their priority is to process them quickly and according to network provider contracts. Your priority likely is more cost driven. They don't allow claims auditing for errors or duplicates. Who made that choice? Not the employer. They like auto-adjudication, you may prefer claims are reviewed or audited for accuracy to avoid overpayment and duplicate charges.

Self-Funding

A self-funded health plan allows the employer to monitor the healthcare supply chain claims data and fixed cost. This is the first step, and it's necessary to improve cost and become proactive in containing cost. A Third Party Administrator (TPA) acts as the insurance company for the employer and manages the healthcare plan. Most self-funding plans are partially self-funded with stop-loss insurance to limit the employer risk while only paying for actual claims. This model is necessary to give the employer the transparency needed to understand the claims data, utilization, and the employer's unique challenges. With this cost-plus strategy the employer pays administration cost plus actual claims.

With transparency the employer will have itemized cost reports for the TPA administration, PPO network, stop-loss insurance, broker fees, pharmacy fees, and of course medical and pharmacy claims. The employer can then see what's going on with the plan, then bring focus on problem areas.

The employer must have the flexibility to work with the administrators or vendors they choose—whether it's medical management, claims management, pharmacy benefits managers (PBM) or network. This freedom of choice also allows employers to change those vendors if they don't perform or choose vendors with more proactive strategies. Without that choice, it's not much different than fully-insured with transparency.

There are many variations of self-funded plans, but they all have the same basic structure. What's important to the employer is that the structure and focus of the plan is what the employer wants and needs. All of the varying options have their strengths, but the strength should match up with the employer's needs.

Self-Insured; Level Funding Premium Plans

Level funded plans have become quite popular, and they offer a good entry into self-funding. They provide claims and utilization reports so employer know where their claims dollars are spent. This type of plan has pre-set structures with limited options, similar to fully-insured. The employer pays the monthly premiums at the maximum funding amount and has a known fixed monthly expense. That known premium is an important consideration to most employers but especially to small employers. The claims are processed and paid from the claims fund. If claims exceed the claims fund the stop-loss carrier pays the overage. At the end of the plan year, any remaining funds belong to the plan. In a fully-insured plan remaining funds belong to the carrier.

Most TPAs offer the level funded option. Several fully-insured carriers now offer this as an alternative to their fully-insured plans. But most of the carriers keep part of the unused claim fund; usually 50 percent.

Carriers are offering this level funding plan to very small employers, with as few as two employees. In addition to claims reporting, the employer avoids most Affordable Care Act (ACA) burdens that impact small employers. As an ERISA plan, they avoid state insurance requirements, community rating, guaranteed issue, and avoid the 2-3 percent state premium taxes. By underwriting the small group medical risk is assessed based on the group and moderately healthy groups enjoy better pricing than ACA guaranteed issue plus claims reports. Even if no funds are returned these groups usually get better rates than ACA fully-insured plans.

Medical Management

All providers and TPAs provide some level of medical management to members of the medical plan. Most medical management and case management teams don't get involved (or avoid involvement) until a precertification for a medical procedure is requested or a member with a chronic illness is driving large claims. Then case management reaches out and gets involved with the member at some level. Case management and disease management are usually specialists such as cancer, cardiac, or dialysis. If the plan member wants any assistance with medical management, it's not always easy to find.

A proactive medical management group will be available when the member calls that number on the back of the card. If the member's primary care doctor tells them to see a cardiologist, the employer wants medical management to direct them to the type of cardiologist that's right for them with high quality standards. In other words, be helpful to the member in a complicated health need. This is a people business, seems obvious. When asking questions about medical management find out if you'll have the same team focused on your members. Having the same medical management team focused on your members appears to be more proactive and informed.

Telehealth Medicine

Telehealth medicine has become very popular over the last five years. It provides a convenient option to members 24 hours a day, 7 days a week when they need routine healthcare. Most instances of allergies, bronchitis, strep throat, UTI, pink eye, sinusitis and earaches can be diagnosed and treated over the phone or Skype. The doctor can write a prescription if necessary and the member can pick up the prescription rather than sitting in an ER, urgent care, or doctor's office full of sick people coughing on them.

It's a useful benefit but it also directly reduces cost to the employer medical plan. About 70 percent of emergency room visits are unnecessary and could have been solved with a phone call to doctor. The member gets immediate medical attention and the employer reduces costs to the medical plan; everyone wins. Place the telehealth phone number on the medical card to remind members about the service and make it convenient to find.

Expert Second Opinion

Expert second opinion is a newer benefit now being offered as a separate employee option by a third party vendor. It can be added to fully-insured plan or included with self-funded plans. It's been available for large 10,000-plus employee companies for years but is now available for even small groups. The benefit is intended to review the more complex, critical, and costly problems and focuses on the right diagnosis and the right treatment.

The noteworthy cost containment point is that 45 percent of the time a second opinion corrects or modifies the diagnosis,

75 percent of the time they correct or modify treatments. Think about the impact that would have on the member and on the plan cost. Case studies show members diagnosed with cancer, scheduled for life-altering surgery that was cancelled because of misdiagnosis in the second opinion.

Reference Base Pricing

One of the more significant cost containment strategies underway today is reference based pricing. While PPO provider network agreements are based on undisclosed pricing, reference based pricing (RBP) normally references established Medicare price at the provider. There is no network with RBP; members can go to any provider they want. The provider must be licensed and accept money for payment; that's it. With PPO contract prices ranging from 200-600 percent of Medicare rate, it's no wonder medical plans want the price determined from a more known, stable Medicare price point. It's also no surprise hospitals prefer the higher PPO networks' prices.

We don't have networks for anything else like buying a car, a house, or clothes so why do we need a network for medical care? The RBP model seems logical and has been around ten years. More important than price is quality of care. With RBP models provider searches also look at price and quality outcomes, infection rates, the quality of care issues that are never talked about with PPO networks.

There are many TPAs who specialize in reference base pricing. Most want to offer hospitals and other providers prices in the 120-150 percent of Medicare rates. Offering providers in the higher 150 percent range will get more acceptance, offering something in the lower range will have more push-back from the providers. Methods differ, so review their process. Understand how they communicate with providers and members. The more communication the TPA has in the pre-certification process for procedures, the better the outcomes. Most review provider quality and cost. They'll help the members find the better quality providers.

Most providers will accept the RBP but the challenge is when they don't and balance bill the members. Understand the how the RBP TPA will handle those issues and they should provide legal representation for the employee. Balance billing is the common objection against RBP. But people forget all the balance billing that goes on with PPO Networks. Members believe they're using PPO in-network providers but find out anesthesiologists, lab work or ER providers are out-of-network and the member is out of luck. Who helps the member then? No one. Every employee meeting we talk about using their PPO network providers and someone has a story about taking two to five years to pay off an out-of-network claim. So don't believe PPO networks do not have balance billing issues.

Member communication is critical. Make a special effort to introduce the RBP process and objectives. Reinforce the strategy from top management and not just human resources, and then, periodically repeat the communications.

Pharmacy Management

Pharmacy benefit manager's (PBMs) manage the medical plan's prescription drugs for both fully-insured and self-insured plans. They're responsible for processing and paying prescription drug claims. But they also maintain the formulary, contracting with pharmacies and negotiate discounts with drug manufactures. Typically, pharmacy cost are 25 percent of a medical plans expense. As the drug prices skyrocket, this cost driver deserves its own special attention. Brand name prescriptions are increasing 13 percent annually, the 50 most popular generic drugs increased 373 percent in the last four years. Specialty pharmaceuticals, the most expensive drugs are increasing over 17 percent annually. And while specialty drugs are a small portion of total drugs (9 of 10 prescriptions filled) they represent about one-third of total cost in 2016 and expect to be 50 percent of drug sales by 2020. Again, this cost driver deserves its own special attention by the plan sponsor.

These large costs and budgets encourage large incentives to manufactures, PBMs, TPAs, insurance companies and even brokers to increase drug prescriptions dispensed. You may expect the PBM would make every effort to contain cost but balance the cost and quality of care in the best interest of the medical plan and their plan participants. But that is actually the exception not the rule. In most plans, there are incentives to fill more prescriptions. When choosing a PBM you must eliminate those incentives to increase cost and align their incentives with the plans sponsor and members. Read the PBM agreement. The pricing and procedures need to be transparent. A fiduciary PBM will only be paid for the transaction and not paid rebates, formulary admin fees, price protection, and any other incentives they may create. One-hundred percent of all third-party revenue should be paid to the plan sponsor.

If your plan does not have a member taking a high cost specialty drug, it will. Be prepared with a PBM and strategy that's aligned with your interest and the members before you're dealing with high cost specialty drugs.

In addition to fiduciary PBMs there are improved options to deal with specialty drugs. Several companies have developed Pharmacy cost-mitigation programs (PCMP) in addition to your PBM. They work with self-insured plans to significantly reduce the cost of maintenance name brand drugs and specialty drugs. Their innovation is simple and straight-forward; they find a lower cost.

With the manufacturer's assistance program many of the drugs can be purchased at zero cost. With the right PBM the international pharmacy program allows them to purchase the prescriptions from Tier 1, English speaking countries United Kingdom, Canada, Australia, and New Zealand at a fraction of the cost. They even have a pharmacy medical tourism program where employees can be paid to travel to the country like Cayman Islands for their prescription treatment, stay at a resort, and still save significant cost to the plan.

While these programs and methods are less convenient than going to the local pharmacy, some plans can save 70-90 percent. The employee gets their expensive prescriptions or treatments and have zero out-of-pocket cost.

It's definitely not the status quo but can be a lifesaving, life changing program for employees. Continuous employee communications is essential so they remember the program when they need it.

Conclusion

Of course, employee buy-in is the key to implementing any new innovative program. They need to know the answers to the obvious questions of "why" and "how" it affects "me." It's a good and compelling story for employees, so keep telling it. Regular and continuous communications will go a long way for employee acceptance.

As the previously described programs are adopted and properly implemented, employers realize substantial cost savings while employees are better engaged in the healthcare buying process, and therefore, consistently achieve better outcomes for themselves.

BRIAN TSCHETTER

Partner
Arizona Benefit Consultants, LLC
Phoenix, Arizona

Brian Tschetter recently joined Arizona Benefit Consultants as a Partner in Phoenix, Arizona. In 2002, Brian founded Compass Benefits Group LLC a benefits consulting firm serving small to mid-size employers in the western United States.

Prior to the benefits business, he worked in the bank card industry with Bank of America as Senior Vice President, Bank Card Marketing and Product Management. He has also served in marketing and product management with Mellon Bank and Michigan National Bank. While at the banks he launched multiple products, strategies, and tactics including repricing multi-billion dollar portfolios to optimize growth and profitability.

Brian has always been driven to find a better way to do things to improve the results. "It's always been done that way" is a red flag of neglect. The status quo of healthcare and the benefits business is overdue to be challenged. There are many new strategies and tactics employers can take to improve employee benefits while reducing cost.

www.abcllc.org
btschetter@abcllc.org
480.661.4776

CHAPTER FIVE

The Patient's Healthcare Decision

*Out of Control Health Insurance Costs
and How to Fix It!*

JEFF HAUDENSCHIELD

Only in the relatively recent past have we had the option to decide where and from whom we could choose our primary physician, specialist, surgeon, or pharmacist. Until the later part of the 20th century, in a mostly rural world and in America, those services were largely performed by the local medical expert who carried most of what he needed, including medicines, in a small black bag. The total cost of care consisted of whatever the doctor charged. In most cases any serious infection, cancer, or other grave condition that the body couldn't handle was fatal. There was not much of a decision to make . . . and you did get what you paid for.

That has all changed with innovation and invention in modern medicine including computer aided surgery, genetically matched cancer fighting drugs and orthopedic surgeries to fix most of the wear and tear on our bodies. The advances in medical technology have mushroomed in the last thirty years and continue at an ever accelerating rate. Costs are also rising exponentially. In some of the first health plans we managed in 1986, I recall employer health plans with Rx premium costs between $1-4 per employee per month (PEPM) and a total medical premium of $60 PEPM! Plans now in 2017-2018 are averaging between $100-$150 PEPM just for Rx and total medical premiums costs average between $400 and $900 PEPM. Below is a chart showing how health insurance premiums and employees contributions toward them have far outpaced workers' earnings and inflation from 1999 to 2016.

PREMIUM INCREASES OUTPACE INFLATION, EARNINGS

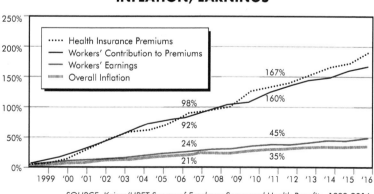

SOURCE: Kaiser/HRET Survey of Employer-Sponsored Health Benefits, 1999-2016. Bureau of Labor Statistics. Consumer Price Index, U.S. City Average of Annual Inflation (April to April). 1999-2016. Bureau of Labor Statistics. Seasonally Adjusted Data from the Current Employment Statistics Survey, 1999-2016 (April to April).

But how do people make these important decisions? Why do some people meticulously research their ailment, considering all the important variables before scheduling their surgeries? Many listen to the advice of the first physician or specialist who offers a diagnosis. Others ask a coworker, friend in healthcare, or other perceived "expert" to help them with this emotional, stressful, and most important decision. These overwhelming and potentially life changing decisions do not come along very often so it is not something anyone can become adept at or comfortable in doing.

The truth is that people decide in every possible way. If they are lucky enough to have an advocate, either a friend or relative or ideally an expert hired by the employer, they will enjoy the benefits of good research and actual reports of the physician who does this procedure the most, who does it best and who does not. This we see as the exception rather than the norm. Most people listen to their friends or family on which surgeon they revere as "the best." While it may be true that he/she really is the most competent, it could very well be the case that another facility is better run with more procedures, fewer infections, fewer re-admittances, etc. It might also be true that the better outcome hospitals are less costly and therefore provide a better overall value for both patient and employer.

Our medical culture in the U.S. lauds freedom for the patient. It is the ultimate fringe benefit. I can choose the best care for myself and get the best surgery, and therefore live my best and longest life possible. That freedom though, has been the last straw for health care costs as it both randomizes choice in the best value provider as well as who can ensure the best outcome. This crapshoot neither works out well for in plan costs nor for patient outcomes. Individuals and groups pay dearly in their premiums because the resultant claims from this non-management of care. Providers aren't incentivized to control those extra costs, as they can represent more revenue/profits for the facility. For instance, in a common employer plan where an employee enjoys an open access PPO medical plan, (s)he could travel to just about any center of excellence for a specific treatment and his/her total cost (except for travel) would be no more than if (s)he checked in to the nearest hospital.

In an alarming but probably all too common recent example of "trusting a provider to refer" gone wrong, it was found that a physician was referring patients to a medical specialist who was his close friend. While this is common and in most cases beneficial, here it was not. As it turned out, this "great doctor" was not board certified in his specialty and, in addition, had sanctions against his license in three different states! These facts were all uncovered through direct engagement and work by the nurse professionals at a medical management partner of ours, and through conversations with a nurse advisor, they were able to offer alternative options to the patient and a promise of a better result. The patient was able to win by averting potential disaster and the employer also won with a healthier employee and by avoiding additional medical plan costs in re-admission, infection, etc.

The other more basic decision one makes is whether to seek out care. Often, economics play a major role, as in, "This deductible is more than I can afford," or, "I'm not able to get there because of my job." Many find drug co-pays unaffordable, especially with more expensive specialty drugs. Others decide to forego care because they are afraid of being diagnosed with something serious and yet others rationalize that it does not run in their family and other excuses. As an example, the cost of not treating diabetes can be devastating both in mortality for the patient and cost to the insurance plan. If left untreated, complications such as heart disease, nerve damage, blindness, kidney failure, and amputations end up costing many multiples in cost vs. patients who control their blood sugar with diet, exercise, and medications.

Rising Deductibles/Co-insurance

Another big factor we have seen in decision making by insureds has been the rapid increase in patient share in cost for treatment, in both the form of deductibles and co-insurance. Not too many years ago, HMO plans with copays for primary physician and for Rx were the only costs a patient would incur no matter the illness, injury, surgery, etc. The deductibles of the 80s, although small, went away for a time and while provider networks were limited to a geographic region, those with limited means were not forced to make decisions based on cost if they had a plan.

As plan costs began to increase in the early 2000s, employers and individuals were forced to make difficult decisions based on premium budgets. Premium share started to shift from employer to employee, especially for family tiers, and deductibles and co-insurance were re-introduced to control costs. These "shared

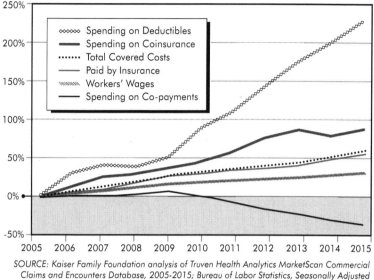

CUMULATIVE INCREASES IN HEALTH COSTS, AMOUNTS PAID BY INSURANCE, AMOUNTS PAID FOR COST SHARING AND WORKERS WAGES, 2005-2015

SOURCE: Kaiser Family Foundation analysis of Truven Health Analytics MarketScan Commercial Claims and Encounters Database, 2005-2015; Bureau of Labor Statistics, Seasonally Adjusted Data from the Current Employment Statistics Survey, 2005-2015 (April to April).

costs" have far outpaced inflation and have also changed the way people with insurance think about going for care. Many group plans saw enrollment drop as employees chose to go without coverage or find a lesser, cheaper plan elsewhere. Many of those without coverage who became sick could then re-enroll in their group plan or in January on an ACA exchange to have their ailment covered. This is called Adverse Selection and it drives rates even higher as a greater percentage of healthy people stay off-coverage.

As can be seen below, the average annual increase in medical deductibles, coinsurance, and premiums has been unsustainable compared with wage growth in the period between 2005 and 2015.

The advent and rise of the Qualified High Deductible Health Plan (Q plans) and their accompanying Health Savings Accounts (HSA) have been another innovative way insurers and employers have shifted costs to the insured and while they are certainly beneficial for the high income and healthy individual, Q plans have been especially financially thwarting when offered to and bought by those with lower income and no liquid assets. These Q plans are particularly difficult for the policyholders who do not fund their HSA account to cover deductible costs and experience a medical event. Q plans mandate that all deductible costs be met before the plan pays anything so the full cost of doctor visits, prescriptions, etc. must be paid until the full deductible is met without the benefit of co-pays. Many employers offer these plans to employees as the only choice and patients do not fully grasp how the plans work until they are facing a crippling bill.

The Affordable Care Act

In 2010, the Affordable Care Act was put into law and it changed the way many people thought about insurance. For anyone who was ill, it was a godsend. There were no medical questions to answer and if you signed up on time and paid your premium, everything was covered. For those with a low income, government subsidies covered most of the premium and in many cases deductibles and co-pays were even lowered.

As you can imagine, for a time this led to a flood of large claims vs. the premium for carriers as they had to digest all of those previously uninsured people. What happened as a result? Premiums rose, plans offered by carriers dwindled and, as a result, those remaining became deductible and co-insurance heavy, and in some cases, carriers stopped offering plans entirely.

On a small group level (less-than 50 or 100 employees depending on the state) plans were now offered only on a community rated basis and rate determining factors were limited to zip code, age, and smoking status. The good health of a group no longer influenced rates and so wellness programs no longer made financial sense for groups to deploy as far as determining premium rates. (We still like the concept of wellness for its morale boost and how they help with productivity and reduced absenteeism). Being healthy should be a goal for everyone for quality of life reasons alone but taking away the financial incentive for small employers to help with employee wellness was a mistake, in my opinion.

What Can Be Done?

Clearly, the government is not going to fix the problem because a working solution would require too much cooperation and compromise. There are too many special interests who are especially vested in continuing the trend of premium rates and provider costs. The only way it can happen is on a grass roots level by the people who do not care more about garnering votes, namely employers.

Recently, Berkshire Hathaway, JP Morgan, and Amazon announced that they were beginning a study on how they could deliver healthcare to their employees in a much more cost-effective manner. Warren Buffet was interviewed by CNBC referred to healthcare costs as "a tapeworm on the economic system." He said that they could achieve three to four percent savings without much effort but that they "were looking for something much bigger than that."[1] From many of the comments Mr. Buffet made in his interview, it sounded to me like he intends on trying to do many of the things we are doing now for clients.

What Are We Doing?

In my business as a benefits specialist, I help employers decide on a strategy in providing health insurance and other benefit plans and show them ways to decrease total costs with various proven strategies. As benefit advisers, we strive to turn this dire situation around for employers, employees, and their families. You may ask, "I thought you worked with the employer to sell them a plan for their employees every year." That used to be an accurate description before premium and plan costs went through the roof and forced everyone to be more creative. Our goal is to make insurance affordable and usable for everyone in the plan through innovative strategies that depend on many factors. We want to help people change the way they decide to access healthcare by first accessing expert guidance.

It starts with education for employees and their families. The first job is to introduce employees to the idea of using an expert with whom they can consult on finding a specialist, answering their Rx questions or managing a disease. A medical management

---

[1] CNBC, Warren Buffett interview, February 26, 2018

expert can help identify the course of action that would give the patient their optimal result and also continuously help through their treatment.

In addition to onsite education and support from their human resources department, there are phone applications available so information can be at everyone's fingertips. It ties everything together and empowers the patient to feel in control of their care options. This app includes a live telephonic doctor to help diagnose and even prescribe medications on the spot, a viable and preferred alternative to the ER in many cases. It links users with trained medical management professionals as well as plan information and more. In this age of technology, employers must help their people communicate the way most of society does now: on their smart phones.

Plan designs alone can also incentivize users to seek out best value options for themselves in elective-surgery situations—these incentives might include waiving the deductible or even offering a bonus for using a better value provider. With significant "large" claims managed in this manner, plan costs are greatly reduced—further helping the employee by putting a halt to their premium increases, and in some cases, result in an overall reduction of costs.

Chronic diseases are often not monitored like they should be. Many who are suffering really do need the help of an outreach from a nurse to help with decisions they need to make on treatment, medication physicians, etc. This proactive engagement can not only save lives but many thousands in unnecessary claim costs.

On the prescription side, there is also much waste going on. Who pays for it? Of course, the poor patients now maxing out their credit cards and having to pay $250 or $500 in separate Rx deductibles or all at once for their specialty medication. As you can imagine, many prescriptions go unfilled every month by those who cannot afford it. Unfilled medications can result in worsening conditions which can lead to severe claims. This is a terrible situation for the employee as well as for the whole group plan. The big-name Pharmacy Benefit Managers (PBMs) are in business to benefit their shareholders, not the group clients for whom they process claims.

On a recent *60 Minutes* episode, the city of Rockford, Illinois, sued their PBM for negotiating a deal with a drug maker for scheming to keep a highly priced drug for a rare disease as its exclusive distributor. The PBM responded to *60 Minutes* by saying it was "not contractually obligated to contain costs."[2] Schemes like this only drive up plan costs, increasing employee premium pay and push up deductibles.

We have found several solutions where an employer can hire a fiduciary PBM to manage the pharmacy contracts with the drug manufacturers. They are hired to process claims for a fixed-cost per claim and are always looking to contain costs for the employer plan who hires them. There are pharmacy plans that go much further in finding discounts by accessing expensive medications in a multitude of ways at greatly reduced prices and in many cases at a fraction of previous plan costs. By

---

[2] CBS, "60 Minutes", May 6, 2018

utilizing different methods, the employer can achieve as much as a 50 percent reduction in their Rx spend. Oh, and co-pays for expensive specialty drugs are also eliminated for the patient, so they do not have the dilemma of whether to buy their drug or groceries for the family.

By protecting the employer's most valuable asset, their employees, both in accessing care and by keeping their pocketbook intact, we help them to succeed in retaining their best talent by keeping the workforce as healthy as they possibly can. This in turn maximizes productivity and profitability for the organization creating a truly sustainable and mutually beneficial long-term relationship in which all parties win.

JEFF HAUDENSCHIELD

Co-Founder
The Benefits Group
Clarks Summit, PA

Jeff Haudenschield has been a healthcare consultant for more than twenty years. He is co-owner of The Benefits Group, where he provides guidance and expert advice to employer groups on how to offer the best benefits to their employees. His primary concentration is with groups of more than 50 employees and he particularly enjoys helping his clients uncover innovative ways to reduce their healthcare spending, while improving the benefit experience for the group, overall.

He began his insurance career in 1985, with The Equitable in Scranton, PA, as a life, health, and investment advisor. Jeff went on to work in a P&C Agency, where he served as manager for a short time. While there helping to build business, the benefits arm grew exponentially. By 2002, it became obvious to him that helping employer groups solve their benefits puzzle was his passion, and, along with his now business partner Jim Blachek, he began his own insurance practice which encompassed group benefits consulting. Jeff and Jim focused their attention to begin growing business throughout Northeastern Pennsylvania.

Today, The Benefits Group has seen excellent growth—up from its initial three employees, the firm is now home to a well-versed staff of sixteen who serve roughly 400 employer benefit group clients located across the country, primarily in the Northeast.

Jeff received his B.S. in Finance from The University of Delaware, class of 85' and resides in Waverly, Pennsylvania with his family.

He currently serves alongside fellow industry-leaders, as a Membership Partner of the NextGen Benefits Mastermind Partnership—an innovative, collaborative group comprised of forward-thinking benefits agency consultants from around the country, leading the way in the next-generation benefits revolution.

www.benegroup.net
jeff@benegroup.net
570.586.1859

CHAPTER SIX

Direct Contracting—A Solid Approach to Savings for Employers

DEKE LAPE & BETH JOHNSON

E very renewal season, we were drowning in a pool of unanswered questions that had to be answered. What are we going to do about higher premiums, disgruntled employers, bewildered employees, and raging medical costs? We knew that we had to do something . . . something really BIG to change the course that the employee benefit industry took. We had to create a benefit system that made *everyone* happy.

Here is the story of what our company, Mitchell Insurance, did to WIN back the employees, employers, and medical systems . . .

After the 2012 fall renewal season, we became tired of the way in which we advised our clients on their employee benefits. In fact, advising may not even be a fair statement. We were simply helping them manage increases from year to year by doing the same old thing: increasing deductibles and copays and passing more cost along to the employee.

We wanted to have something better to offer—something that was different and could make a difference for our clients. We wanted an innovative idea that we could put in front of a prospective client to differentiate us from the current broker who was most likely just doing the same thing we had done for years: managing the account from year to year and crossing fingers that rates wouldn't go up too much. This old way of doing business was unsustainable for us and, even more importantly, our clients. *Something* had to change!

Our first step was developing a direct contract with our local hospital system, Missouri Delta Medical Center (MDMC), that we could offer to clients and prospects. Ironically, the MDMC administration had been discussing the exact same thing, so the mutual timing of the idea couldn't have been better.

The contract, called "Top Tier Contract," was ready to roll out in the latter part of 2013 for groups that had renewal dates of January 1, 2014, or later. We began marketing the idea to some existing groups and prospects. In doing so, we found a high level of interest, excitement, and curiosity for it. We were able to include four client organizations into our Top Tier by January 1, 2014.

By late 2014 we had collected enough claim information on the participating groups to compare to prior years and the performance of the plans became visibly apparent . . . THIS NEW APPROACH WAS WORKING!

All three parties involved in the Top Tier Contract—the employee, employer, and medical system—benefited from the direct connection to the local hospital. It became clear that this model had many benefits for all parties involved. In the following three sections we will explain how the employee, employer, and hospital/provider have all prospered.

Part 1: The Employee

Analyzing our old approach, we realized that more often than not we left out the most important piece of a health plan—the *people*. Instead, we focused on the deductible, copays, prescription plan, or max out-of-pocket. While these things are certainly important, they don't compare to the most important piece of the equation. How could we ever expect to set up a successful employee benefit plan if we didn't include the *people* in the discussion, explaining to them how the plan works, why it works, and how they are the biggest piece of the puzzle?

The employees and their dependents have to understand every aspect of their plan so that they can become a part of the solution to make it successful for them. For this evolution to take place, we now realize that our job is to be transparent and to simplify the details that are often confusing and frustrating to employees. Our clients' employees must understand their health plan and know that they are at the center of the Top Tier Contract.

First, we design a plan that incentivizes the employee to access care at facilities who have agreed to be part of our program. We do that by significantly reducing the deductible and maximum out-of-pocket exposure if the employee utilizes the facilities within the Top Tier network. While a reduction in out-of-pocket costs is something that is easy for an employee to understand, it still takes some re-training and educating to make sure they understand how it works. Over the years, we have done a disservice to our industry by setting up plans that do not offer valuable incentives to employees. The difference in cost from facility to facility can be in excess of 500 percent, but the employee has never been incentivized to find the best value when seeking care. Why wouldn't we want to reduce the deductible and maximum out-of-pocket for employees who make a decision to have a procedure done at a facility that could potentially save their plan thousands and thousands of dollars? It's really common sense, but this simply isn't being done.

Second, we make sure we give the employees and their dependents benefits and opportunities to be part of the solution. One example is a diabetes value-based benefit. With diabetes growing at such a rapid rate, it is clearly one of the biggest claim drivers on our plans. Unfortunately, many medical plans are simply setting up members to fail by having benefits in place that make staying compliant with medication too expensive. We have eliminated that by having a benefit in place that allows employees to access diabetes medication and supplies at zero charge with no copay if they comply with the drug formulary set forth in the plan design. While this action definitely costs our plans some claims dollars up front, it is a saver on the back end because more and more of our members are compliant with their medication, thus reducing the risk of major claims down the road—not to mention the impact of a healthier workforce!

In summary, the employees have to be made to feel like they are able to make a difference in how much their medical plan ultimately costs and what type of benefits they are offered by their employer. Employees are part of the solution by making good decisions on when and where they receive their care. The employer is putting a plan design in place that allows the employee to take advantage of reduced out-of-pocket exposure and first-dollar benefits all in an effort to eliminate the financial barrier our flawed system has created for someone to receive the care they need when they need it.

Part 2: The Employer

It's no secret that employers have been struggling mightily with the cost of their medical plans. As stated in the beginning, the strategy has basically been to shift cost by raising deductibles, copays and the maximum out-of-pocket limits or just simply by increasing the employee contribution to the plan. Then, we cross our fingers and hope for a renewal offer that is not worse than the one a year ago. We know this because we have lived it with our clients. So, how does the employer win in this new model?

The obvious answer is that the employer wins because the employees are going to seek care at facilities that charge less for their services. We know the employee is going to take advantage of this opportunity because they are heavily incentivized through the plan design to seek their care at participating top tier facilities. When the employees do that, the cost of claims goes down dramatically and the medical plan is impacted in a very positive way. This is all true, and even by itself this is probably enough to make the employer win. However, the impact of this can be felt much deeper within each organization than simply in the medical plan cost.

If employers are able to flatten out or reduce what they spend on employee benefits, then positive reactions begin to take place within their organization:

- Net profit
- Employee wages
- Hiring of new employees
- Capital expenditures to increase productivity and sales

This list can go on and on, but it's a fact that the amount of money spent on benefits within organizations has been suffocating.

What are they getting in return in the current system?

- Confused and frustrated employees
- A non-transparent system in which employees have no idea of the cost of care from one place to another
- Limited claim data on their groups that makes it difficult to assess the needs of the employees and the direction they should go as a company

If an employer is going to have benefits be their second or third-largest line item in their budget, don't they deserve some kind of return on the investment? We want the plan to be a tool for attracting and retaining talented employees. The medical plans should be designed to allow the employees to access care with reduced up-front cost. This makes the employees happy and gives them the ability to get the care they need to help keep them healthy. The attitude of the employees becomes infectious in the work place in a positive way instead of a negative way.

Employers love happy employees. When employers are investing the amount of money they are investing in benefits, they **deserve** some ROI. The plan designs for the employee and the contracts we have in place with medical facilities deliver ROI. So, while employers win on the cost of claims, they are also benefiting from taking something that has been a frustrating experience for the employee and turning it into a positive experience.

Part 3: The Hospital/Provider

Many hospitals and providers are struggling mightily and are fighting hard for your business, for new patients, and for the privilege of helping you with your labs, x-rays, procedures, and any other medical needs that may arise. Most hospitals have come to the realization that they can't grow their income by raising prices, so their only real opportunity to grow revenue is by gaining market share. Not only do they want more market share, but they also want the most profitable market share. Hospitals desperately want their customers to be insurance-paying customers, as the reimbursement levels for the care they provide is typically much higher than that of Medicare and Medicaid. Under our direct contracting model, this is where the medical provider not only sacrifices but also wins.

The sacrifice made by the provider is the lowering of their cost of care. The amount of that reduction can vary from provider to provider, but it is always developed as a percentage of Medicare. We want to develop the contract in that manner because it gives us an actual number that is known. This is in contrast to how insurance companies and providers show discounts in the PPO model. They will tout to insurance brokers and clients that if you go to certain providers, you will receive a 50 percent discount. Well, that may sound pretty good, but the question that needs to be asked is, "Fifty percent of what amount?" The current system simply isn't transparent enough for consumers to make an educated decision on what a medical facility is charging and where to get care.

The provider wins because in return for their reducing cost as described above, we are designing plans that steer the employees to the participating facilities. As described in the prior section, the employees are flocking to these facilities because their out-of-pocket exposure has been tremendously reduced. As a result, the hospitals are gaining the market share they desire, and this is generating more revenue for the participating facility.

Hospitals and providers also tend to have issues with their accounts receivable and being able to successfully collect the money owed to them by their patients, which are the employees. The vast majority of employer-sponsored medical plans have plan designs with high deductibles and max out-of-pockets. The maximum exposure for the employee often exceeds $6,000 per person insured. While this sometimes isn't a large amount when compared to the entire cost of a procedure, it is a tremendous amount of money to employees living paycheck to paycheck, which is the case with most Americans. These types of plan designs make it extremely hard for the provider to collect the employee portion of the cost of the claim, forcing many of them to make arrangements for the patients to pay their balance over a long period of time. With our model, we have changed the plan designs to make it much more affordable for the employee to visit these facilities, thus making it easier for the provider to collect the money that is due to them.

Since we started working on this almost five years ago, we continue to strive to learn more about how we can do our part to help improve a system that simply isn't sustainable. In our experience, it is much easier to make progress when you have the employee, the employer, and medical facility all working together to find a solution. As we continue down this road, there are still improvements that need to be made, but we are happy to say it has been a model that has brought people together in a sincere effort to improve delivery of healthcare to the employees of the companies that make communities thrive at the medical facilities that are vital to our community. ***Win, Win, Win!!***

DEKE LAPE

Employee Benefits Consultant, Partner
Mitchell Insurance, Inc.
Sikeston, MO

Deke Lape is an employee benefits consultant with Mitchell Insurance, Inc., and also serves as the secretary/treasurer of the corporation. Deke has 20 years of experience in the employee benefits insurance and counseling/brokerage field. He has worked with employers of many industries, including manufacturing, not-for-profits, municipalities, education, and healthcare. He has extensive experience in both fully-insured and self-funded medical plan arrangements, consumer-driven plans, and worksite and ancillary benefits.

Deke is a 1997 graduate of the University of Missouri—Columbia. Since then, he has been active in his community as a member of St. Francis Xavier Church and serving on the Board of Directors of Missouri Delta Medical Center, YMCA of Southeast Missouri Board of Directors (past chairman), Sikeston Public Schools board of education (past president), and Sikeston Jaycees (past president). Deke and his wife, Jill, reside in Sikeston with their children Jay and Will.

mitchellhealth180.com
dlape@mitchellinsinc.com
573.471.0538

BETH JOHNSON

Employee Benefits Consultant, Partner

Mitchell Insurance, Inc.
Sikeston, MO

Beth Johnson is an employee benefits adviser and President of Mitchell Insurance Inc. As a healthcare strategist and consultant for nearly 25 years, Beth has a demonstrated history of reducing employer healthcare spend by creating partnerships between employers and local healthcare systems to bring about real change in how employees view and utilize their health plan. She has proven track record working with a variety of industries of eliminating barriers to care so employees receive the right care, at the right time, in the right place for the right price.

Beth is a 1992 Cum Laude graduate of the University of Missouri-Columbia. She is an active member in her community and currently serves as Vice-Chairman of the Missouri Delta Medical Center Board of Directors, is a past member of the Sikeston Area Chamber of Commerce Board of Directors and past Girl Scout troop leader. As a member of St. Francis Xavier Catholic Church, she is a current board member and past-president of the Parish School Board. Beth and her husband, Joe, reside in Sikeston with their children David and Kathleen.

mitchellhealth180.com
bjohnson@mitchellinsinc.com
573.471.0538

CHAPTER SEVEN

Not All "Voluntary" Benefit Firms Are Alike

How to Save Your HR Team Time and Increase the Employee's Financial Bottom-line

ERIK NAGENGAST

I f you are like most employers, you are offering "voluntary" benefits for one of the following reasons:

- Your medical broker has recommended it
- Your employees have requested it
- You were approached by a "voluntary" benefits agent to offer it

Every year you are faced with the decision whether to raise the cost of health coverage or increase the employee's financial exposure.

Recently, we performed a benefits assessment with a hospital's Vice President of HR and the Director of Benefits. They both agreed that their health benefits played a significant role in an employee's longevity with their company. After hearing that, we asked a follow-up question:

> *Do you believe that "voluntary" benefits play any role in*
> *your employees' satisfaction with their benefits package*
> *and longevity at your company?*

They both responded "NO" quickly elaborating "that in their 22 years (of work), they have never thought that 'voluntary' benefits played such a role." Their statement as to the importance of "voluntary" benefits in their employees' lives was enlightening. It was no surprise why the employees' "voluntary" benefit participation was only about 25 percent of the workforce.

In contrast, our clients normally see involvement at 75 percent of the employee population. I believe one of the causes was that there wasn't a correct understanding by the HR Team as to the significance of "voluntary" benefits to their employees.

In short, these benefits protect the employees and their families from financial peril when an unexpected medical event strikes. Merely having quality medical insurance is no longer enough. There are caps and gaps in the coverage that is only discovered after an event. In addition, the disruption to a household's income due to missed work fuels this financial fire.

Because our firms facilitate the claims process with our policyholders, we have seen thousands of families keep their financial "heads above water" through the protection these plans afford.

"Voluntary" Benefits Are More Than Just Another Benefit

These plans are affordable benefits paid to a policyholder during a medical crisis. They allow the recipient to maintain a reasonable standard of living. Often, they are used to pay for things not covered by the medical insurance.

Here are a few facts showing the difficulty an employee faces with an unexpected financial challenge:

- A survey by Bankrate.com concluded that 60 percent of employees would be in trouble if they had an unexpected $500 auto repair or $1000 emergency room visit.[1]
- It has been documented that eight in 10 employees live paycheck to paycheck.[2]

[1] https://www.bankrate.com/pdfs/pr/20170112-January-Money-Pulse.pdf
[2] https://www.entrepreneur.com/article/313064

- Fifty-seven percent of Americans have less than $1,000 in their savings account, and 39 percent have no savings at all.[3]
- Employer-paid disability, while provided to cover 60 percent of the employee's wages, often amounts to just 40-45 percent after taxes are paid. Benefit caps can make this amount even less.

Let's consider the financial resources an employee would tap into in case of a medical emergency:

Savings Account: This is an option very few employees have built up over time. In fact, six out of 10 people have access to less than $1,000 in their savings account. This is further supported in that only about 41 percent say that they would access their savings.[4] Since eight out of 10 live paycheck to paycheck, there isn't much left to save.

Retirement/Investment Account: Early access to funds in many cases includes a 20 percent penalty. Also, there are often taxes that may have to be paid. So, removing $100 from these accounts may only result in $50-$60 after taxes and penalties.

---

[3]   https://www.cnbc.com/2017/09/14/how-much-money-the-average-millennial-has-in-savings.html

[4]   https://www.bankrate.com/pdfs/pr/20170112-January-Money-Pulse.pdf

Credit Cards: About 21 percent say they would use a credit card to finance their unexpected expense.[5] The average interest rate on a credit card in the United States is *15.96 percent.*[6] Financing the debt can cause strain on the household for years to come.

Family and Friends: Although many would like to help, they are not in a financial position to drain their resources and expose themselves financially.

Paycheck Advance from Employer: Though it exists, fewer and fewer employers offer such a service to their workforce.

"Voluntary" benefits can make a dramatic impact on the employee's ability to pay their bills along with covering additional medical expenses. Over the years our firm has processed tens of thousands of claims for our policyholders. We observe first-hand how they use the funds to help pay their mortgage/rent, auto payment, utility bills, groceries, COBRA, fuel, additional child care, and much more. Simply put, there is a financial chasm between an employee having the resources to pay their bills when their primary source of cash flow is interrupted. "Voluntary" benefits are the bridge that is not only affordable but also accessible with the right strategy.

---

[5] https://www.bankrate.com/pdfs/pr/20170112-January-Money-Pulse.pdf
[6] https://www.creditkarma.com/credit-cards/i/average-apr-on-credit-card/

Voluntary Benefits vs. Ancillary Benefits vs. Enhanced Benefits

Perhaps you have noticed that I have been placing the "voluntary" in quotation marks. This has been for a good reason. It seems that these benefits are most often referred to as either "voluntary" or "ancillary" benefits. These interchangeable terms are used to generally define the following plans: Accident, Cancer, Critical Illness, Hospital, Life, and Disability.

Ancillary Benefits

According to the American Heritage Dictionary, the definition of the word "ancillary" is "of secondary importance; subordinate." It is just offered to employees as something "extra." Because of that, many employees don't take the time to understand how the benefits work with their medical coverage. In my opinion, "ancillary" benefits should only be used to describe items like discounts on gym memberships or restaurants.

Voluntary Benefits

According to the American Heritage Dictionary, the definition of the word "voluntary" is something "done or undertaken of one's own free will." However, it is confusing, because isn't the participation in the "core" benefits (medical, dental, vision) also voluntary?

Enhanced Benefits

According to the American Heritage Dictionary, the definition of the word "enhance" is "to improve or augment, especially in the effectiveness, value, or attractiveness." Bingo! This is only achievable with the correct strategy of how these benefits work <u>with the medical plans</u>. An "enhanced" benefits advisor not only assesses the current medical options, but they also work with various carriers to build the correct "enhanced" benefits for your group.

The brokers that merely "pull a plan off of a shelf" aren't providing an adequate strategy that reflects how these plans work along with the medical coverage. If employees aren't educated about the importance and the place that these benefits have in their coverage, there is a problem.

Remember, about 80 percent of us live paycheck to paycheck and having an unexpected medical event without "enhanced" benefits is like Philippe Petit walking between the Twin Towers without a safety net.[7] It can be done, but is it really worth the risk?

Custom Strategies and Plan Designs Are Essential

Trim the Fat

Are your plans custom to your company and your company's medical plan or are they merely "shelf" plans? I make a distinction here because "shelf" plans often have a large amount of "fat" built into them that doesn't benefit the employee. It is

---

[7]   https://www.theguardian.com/culture/gallery/2015/oct/01/
philippe-petit-walk-between-twin-towers

also essential to determine if any features reward the employee for seeking treatment at costlier medical facilities unnecessarily.

We recently reviewed an accident plan for a prospective client. The plan had a feature that paid **more benefits** to the employee if they went to an emergency room versus an urgent care or primary doctor! As an employer, do you want your employees being financially enticed to seek treatment at an ER when they simply could have gone to their primary care doctor or urgent care? Did your current broker explain that the accident plan had this feature that incentivized employees to the emergency room?

Probably the most "fattening" of all of the benefits is the infamous "wellness" benefit built into an accident plan. I refer to this item as merely a mail-in-rebate. This benefit pays if one goes for their annual physical or some other preventive exam. While on the surface this seems to be a good thing, you must understand that our experience over 25 years and thousands upon thousands of policyholders tell us that <u>only about a third of employees claim this benefit</u>. While many of them are annually receiving their physical, most of them are not claiming this benefit that they are paying for. We build accident plans with richer more cost-effective features, rather than include mail-in-rebates that don't benefit the employee when they need it most.

I need to make a distinction in that "wellness" benefits included with a critical illness plan <u>are necessary</u>. These wellness benefits remind an employee of the importance of critical illness related preventive exams. Early detection is paramount when fighting these diseases. The medical experience is also far better if a critical illness is detected early. By the way, did you know that enhanced benefits can be built to help shrink the medical costs of an employee group?

Designs That Work

When considering the following plans, it is crucial to understand how they're built and how they benefit your employees. Here are a few examples:

Cancer Plan: Recently we were diagnosing the effectiveness of a Cancer Plan and how it worked with cancer care in 2018. Presently most treatments are handled on an outpatient basis with the most significant costs falling into radiation and chemo, experimental therapies, prescriptions, surgeries, and bone marrow and stem cell treatments. One of the employees showed us their chemo treatment bill that amounted to about $7,000 for a week's worth of treatment. Their existing cancer plan only paid them $200 per day with a maximum benefit of $800 a month. We were able to upgrade the plan to one that paid dollar-for-dollar the cost of the chemo services up to $10,000 annually. By the way, it was about the same price as what the employee was paying before.

Long-Term Care: Does your company offer any long-term care? This is our most requested benefit. The advancements in medicine are causing the average person to live longer and the additional care needed is a tremendous financial challenge. Whether medical care is received in a facility or at one's own home, the average person is not prepared for the expense. Here are some facts from the U.S. Department of Health and Human Services:[8]

- The average cost for a semi-private room in a nursing home is $6,844 a month.
- The average cost for a private room in a nursing home is $7,698 a month.
- The average cost for an assisted living facility is $3,628 a month.
- The average cost for a homemaker are $20 per hour and $20.50 per hour for a health aide.

Do you offer anything to help an employee protect themselves and their future? Is the coverage currently provided guaranteed-issue and has the rate stability to avoid future increases? If you are not offering a long-term care solution, now is the time to find out about the strategies that can be implemented for your employees. By the way, how much of your employees' 401(k) will be "chewed up" by their future long-term care needs? Doesn't it make sense if you offer a 401(k) that you should also offer long-term care?

Increase Employee Access to Participate

Generally, most enhanced benefits are offered pre-tax and are only available annually during the open enrollment. While this is widely practiced, it does not benefit the employee. With

---

[8]   https://longtermcare.acl.gov/costs-how-to-pay/costs-of-care.html

most open enrollments occurring in November and December each year, there are far too many distractions for an employee's focus on something so critical. Also, many employees contact our offices inquiring about these coverages after an incident happens to someone they know or love. Their aunt had been diagnosed with cancer, someone in their church was killed in a car accident, a teammate on his or her child's sports team was injured during a game; these are just a few examples of calls we received last week in our offices.

We strongly advocate for employees to participate year-round with enhanced benefits. Structured correctly, this availability does not add more work to the company's HR or payroll. Employees can have the time and ability to meet with our enhanced benefits advisors during the ongoing meetings being held many times throughout the year.

Even though an employee can cancel at any time with this strategy, our persistence level is between one and two percent. That means 98-99 percent continue their coverage year-after-year.

The only way a year-round enrollment works in favor of the employee is if the guaranteed-issue features are also available year-round. There are no "gotcha" items that demand the employee enroll to qualify for the one-time offer of guaranteed-issue. The right enhanced benefits partner can structure this year-round access to benefit the employees while not increasing work on the employer.

Savings to the Employer's Healthcare Budget Is Possible

The employer's bottom-line is an essential piece to the strategy of an enhanced benefits firm. As previously mentioned, an accident plan should incentivize an employee to seek treatment at their primary care or urgent care. There should be no financial incentive to be treated at an ER when other solutions will suffice. Currently the average ER visit costs $1,917 which is 31 percent higher than what it was in 2016.[9]

Also, the hospital plan should include a $0 copay for telemedicine. This will help drive the use of services that do not count toward the employer's medical claims experience. How many visits can be saved with the right enhanced benefits firm driving these messages on your behalf to impact employee care? Enhanced benefits have a financial value directly to the employee and that benefit message can make a difference for the employer.

Service, Service, Service

Benefits are only as good as they are accessible. Unlike medical insurance, enhanced benefits are much more personal. They are more personal in that the policyholder files their claim and receives the funds in their bank account or mailbox. They are involved every step of the way. That is why we make sure to ask every employer during a benefits assessment, what claims services their existing broker provides the employees? In almost all cases, the companies that use their medical broker for the "voluntary"

---

[9] https://money.cnn.com/2018/03/19/news/economy/emergency-room-er-bills/index.html

benefits receive no claims service. For employees to have the best enhanced benefits experience, there must be service provided by the broker to employees and their claims.

It is the responsibility of the employer to know what measures their broker has in place to assist employees with claims. Almost all brokers point the employee to the customer service of the insurance company. <u>That is not enough</u>. The easy part is selling the coverages—the hard part is the service after the sale. The service makes all the difference for an employee and their family. The claims challenges employees face are often unreported to HR.

Over our 23-plus years of providing these benefits and support services to policyholders, we know that 30 percent of claims would not be paid correctly or at all without our help.

Alignment of Purpose with the Employer

Service to the employer is as essential as service to the employee. The HR and payroll teams are often burdened with continuing to provide quality work with shrinking staff to handle their expanding responsibilities.

HR personnel tell us regularly that the previous broker handling the enhanced benefits assured them that these benefits are "free," since "they don't cost the employer anything!" While it is true that there often are no "hard costs" to the employer, it is not true that there are zero costs!

Hard Costs: The employer is paying something toward the benefit. Medical insurance has hard costs for the employer since it's partially or fully-funded by the company.

Soft Costs: These costs are most often calculated by the amount of workforce needed to administer the benefits of the group. They exist in the following ways:

- HR has to reconcile the bill for each of the carriers monthly.
- HR has to resolve employee service issues with the carriers as necessary.
- HR has to update the carriers when an employee has a life-event change.
- HR is involved with notifying the carriers of an employee profile change.
- HR is involved with providing new employees the benefits information.
- Payroll has multiple payroll deductions to manage for several different carriers.
- Payroll has to reconcile premium refunds to employees from the carriers.

Is your HR or payroll teams performing any of these tasks? Are they managing more than a few of these duties? How many hours are spent handling these responsibilities?

Of course, there are costs involved with administering the enhanced benefits. Our firm doesn't hide from that statement.

<u>The difference is that employers should not expect to have to cover
those costs.</u> For instance, our support team handles all of those
duties and absorbs the costs on behalf of our employer-partners.
You need to ask yourself whether your broker does the
following:

- Do they handle 100 percent of the billing reconciliation
  at no cost to you?
- Do they handle 100 percent of the claims assistance for
  employees at no cost?
- Does your broker provide a streamlined single deduction
  bill to payroll at no cost?
- Does your broker handle all premium refunds to employees outside of payroll?

These services are essential to a healthy enhanced benefits
strategy. The efforts of the HR and payroll teams are better spent
in more productive ways. What projects could be tackled by HR
that would benefit the company? What money could be saved
and used in more critical directives?

Conclusion

There is an undeniable connection between an employee's health
and their wealth. When an unexpected medical emergency occurs,
the wealth of the employee is jeopardized. The 401(k) program
that the employee may have been contributing to year-after-year
can be wiped out in an instant. It is critical that they have access
to responsible enhanced benefits at a sensible price.

Our mantra is for an employee to take an hour's pay a week and protect themselves financially. Whether someone makes $10 an hour or $100 an hour, a single hour is something everyone can afford. If someone cannot afford a single hour's pay, they are the ones that need these protections the most!

When you review your partnership with your existing broker, it is most important to reflect on what services they are providing your team and your employees. The insurance carrier(s) selected are secondary to the primary issue. Do you have the right Enhanced Benefits Firm as a partner?

It is the responsibility of the enhanced benefits firm to identify the best carrier(s) for your group's needs.

Here are a few final thoughts to help you determine if your existing broker is delivering the best results:

- Do they regularly move the business every couple of years to new carriers? If so, are they performing a "commission-grab" at the expense of your company and employees.

- Do they provide any assistance to employees when a claim needs to be submitted? If not, then what services are they providing? These important coverages are purchased for the sole purpose of financial protection. If accessing a claim benefit while they are sick or hurt is difficult, then what is the point of the coverage? An employer would not continue to pay fees to a medical broker that did not produce results or provide value. Why should the employer allow the "voluntary" benefits broker to receive commissions for no results or value either?

- Do they have the carrier representative handle the meetings and enrollments instead of their agency? Do they make your staff handle the benefits meetings? If so, they are not connecting with your employees to understand their needs at the grass roots level.

- Do they push all customer service and claims service to the carrier? Having a support team to facilitate an enhanced benefits claim is the most important thing a broker-partner can do for your employees.

- Do they regularly visit their principal carrier-partners' headquarters to build relationships and strategize better solutions? This is crucial to the health of the groups and their longevity.

- Do they meet with your HR and payroll team several times throughout the year to understand new challenges and also any problematic issues? Understanding the changing needs of your company is vital to the health of the partnership and the benefits program.

- Do they provide a consolidated bill and bill reconciliation at no cost to you? Providing the best solutions from various carriers while reducing strain on your staff is a win-win for everyone.

The importance of selecting an enhanced benefits partner is as critical as choosing your core benefits partner. The solutions and strategies they provide protect your most valuable asset— your employees.

ERIK NAGENGAST

Vice President
Lifestyle Benefits
Greater Detroit & Tampa

President
Solutions N Sync
Tampa & Greater Detroit

President
AmeriWorks Financial
Tampa & Greater Detroit

Erik began his benefits career at Lifestyle Benefits when he was still in college. While there he learned from his father the most important part of a successful business is superior service. In 2012 he opened Solutions N Sync to provide benefits, HR, and technology strategies to small and mid-sized businesses. After many successful years of growth he returned to Lifestyle Benefits and took on the additional role of Vice President.

Lifestyle Benefits is a leader in the Enhanced Benefits industry. Providing a quality service experience to both employees and employers is at the core of its philosophy. It specializes in groups that include government, manufacturing, hospital systems, education, and labor unions. Many of these large organizations have been clients for over 20 years with 10,000+ claims processed in-office.

Erik is also the President of AmeriWorks Financial, a third-party administrator, specializing in providing billing solutions to large organizations. Relieving the burden and stress on HR and Payroll Teams is at the center of its focus.

erik@mylifestylebenefits.com
mylifestylebenefits.com
800.219.4843 x110

enagengast@solutionsnsync.com
solutionsnsync.com
866.456.9262 x110

enagengast@ameriworksfinancial.com
ameriworksfinancial.com

CHAPTER EIGHT

Employee Empowerment Through Enrollment Events

How to Enhance Open Enrollment Without Increasing Your Workload

CHRIS WOLPERT

I n recent years many organizations have been embracing an employee-centric philosophy that seeks to develop employee engagement through company culture and team building. Today's empowered workforce values flexibility and freedom. These 21st century employees have in turn rewarded those innovative employers with their loyalty.

> *What employees really want is to be treated like a human being in the workplace, rather than a cog in a machine. Therefore the organization that sees their people as whole, complete people with experiences at work and at home that combine to make a meaningful life. Through the human workplace, employees have access to the experiences that lead to higher job satisfaction and better performance.*
>
> —MetLife Employee Benefit Trends Study 2018

Currently, there's a significant disconnect between how organizations and their people view the delivery of their benefits communication. Employees don't engage in the open enrollment process, which leads to confusion and dissatisfaction with the overall package that is offered. If they don't like the benefit plan, that's just one more reason for them to begin to look for a new place to work.

With websites like Glassdoor.com and Indeed.com, it's also easy for your qualified candidates to eliminate your organization from consideration during their job hunt. That's a real problem, especially considering that the benefit spend is typically one of your organization's top-three expenses on the Profit & Loss statement.

What Role Do Benefits Play?

The annual open enrollment process is when employees become consumers of your benefit plan offerings. Like all other areas of your benefit plan there's a Status Quo way, and a NextGeneration method that increases engagement and improves employee satisfaction.

Ask yourself for a moment . . .

- Why do you offer benefits?
- Do people understand the choices available to them?
- Do they have *choices*, or simply *a* choice?

In the past you've no doubt raised the deductible and increased the employee contribution in order to offset a large increase, but have you ever considered the open enrollment event to be contributing to low employee satisfaction when it comes to your benefit plan?

So how do we zero in on what employees actually *want* from their benefit plan, empower them to select options based on their specific priorities *and* make the process so easy, they can complete the enrollment in a matter of minutes?

In short, how can we make *benefits* live up to their name again?

The Status Quo Enrollment Event

First, let's take a look at an annual event that is a constant source of tension among your employees. Whether you realize it or not, you've been part of a status quo enrollment event in the past.

As an executive team you've already done all the hard work of meeting with several brokers, exchanged numerous emails, evaluated insurance carriers, poured over plan designs, contemplated contribution formulas, and finally, picked what seemed to be the *least-bad* option. Since there was a lot of time consuming *activity* that led up to this open enrollment naturally your employees are going to be very pleased with the plans being offered and completely understand their options after the group meeting, right?

While you may have entered the annual open enrollment meeting with high expectations, it probably didn't go exactly as you'd envisioned. In the back of your mind you knew the plan changes would be unpopular, but you see this event as something you "just need to get through." The renewal deadline was approaching quickly and you had to make a decision to ensure your coverage would continue. Sadly the open enrollment meeting was most likely perceived by your employees as something more reminiscent of a Dunder Mifflin conference room gathering led by Michael Scott from the hit NBC show *The Office*.

Your employees show up first thing in the morning (many still half-asleep) to hear about the changes to your benefit plan for the coming year. While you cross your fingers that your people won't notice healthcare costs are going up yet again, while their take-home-pay remains stagnant. Everyone crowds around in a packed conference room or huddles together around the shop floor to listen to how the benefits have been reduced, while the cost have gone up. It's only a matter of time before your employees will be pounding on your office door complaining and asking for explanations.

Again, this is one of your top tools for recruiting and retaining quality employees, as well as a top expense on your P&L statement.

How the Status Quo Event Harms Your Employees

There are several reasons why these events actually do more harm than good. Study after study has shown that the top causes of open enrollment frustration among employees are:

1. Constant changes to the plans each year (never for the better)
2. Information that is too difficult to understand (with no help to understand it)
3. Being rushed through an already hurried process

So what happens when employees leave feeling confused? They begin to consult *each other* on something nobody *really* understands.

Yikes.

You may have considered offering some alternative options such as enhanced benefits, but it would have been "too hard" or "too much" for your employees to understand. The problem is, they simply haven't been given the opportunity or the tools to *truly* make decisions for themselves when it comes to their own priorities and benefit selections.

They haven't *engaged* in the process, because they haven't been part of it.

We need to get to know more about your employees, who are much more than simply a row on an Excel spreadsheet. It's time to take a step back and think about how congruity can be created in the inadequate enrollment process.

The Next-Generation Enrollment Event

Advancements in technology and systems are always a threat to the Status Quo. Fortunately, there are new innovative cutting-edge processes for benefits administration and open enrollment engagement. These systems not only allow you to communicate the value of these programs at the annual open enrollment, but throughout the entire plan year. Integrated mobile applications allow for employees to view their benefits, plan summaries, and payroll deductions online from anywhere, at any time. Plus the apps contain links to specialty vendors such as telemedicine, medical care advocates, prescription discounts, etc.

Picture this . . .

The afternoon before your open enrollment event starts, each of your employees receive a text message notifying them about some excited changes coming to their benefits plan. Also within that text is a link to a schedule which they can click on to find a time to meet with a benefit counselor. A few minutes later, employees receive a "ringless" voicemail message from a live human that shows up automatically in their voicemail box. In the message, your employees learn they are going to have the opportunity to meet one-on-one with a benefit counselor who is going to explain the changes of the new health plan. They'll also help your employees understand how to download and use the mobile app to access insurance information and connect with their medical advocate nurse directly who will assist them in accessing the right medical care, at the right time, *and* at the right price. If that weren't enough, your employees also learn that they get to go on a "benefits shopping spree" with a defined contribution that puts *them* in the driver's seat to choose the non-medical benefits most important for their situation.

While face-to-face sessions may not be something you've ever considered doing in the past, there is no doubt they are the most *personalized* option. The strongest communication tool human beings have at our disposal is face-to-face. No matter how advanced our technology becomes, there is nothing that's quite the same as making eye contact, shaking hands, and reading body language of someone sitting right across from you.

For an employee, they now have the ability to ask their deeply personal and detailed health questions in a confidential private setting. In an intimate one-on-one setting your employees will have the confidence to share their concerns, while learning about your plan, how it works, and how enhanced benefit options can provide additional protection. Consider using face-to-face sessions for an open enrollment *and* when onboarding new hires.

Enhanced Benefits have become as integral to your overall package as your core offerings (medical, dental, and vision). Gone are the days of voluntary "product dump" programs. Only to watch your rep leave the business within six months. Enhanced benefit carriers have responded to the market by offering pre-tax complementary plans (accident, critical illness, and hospital indemnity) that seek to fill the growing void between stagnant wages and increasing medical deductibles. These plans offer flexibility to both employers and employees in terms of who pays the premium. One of the greatest hidden advantages however, is that when a claim occurs, it's the *employee* who collects tax-free money at a time when they need it most!

For your employees, it's priceless.

Here are five ways to meet employees where they are:[1]

1. When employers offer a ***breath of benefit*** options, they can help alleviate the anxiety that comes with the integration of work-life and home-life.

---

[1] MetLife Employee Benefit Trends Study 2017

2. When employers deliver **_tailored solutions_**, they help an increasingly diverse workforce find the security it's looking for.

3. When employees have access to **_the right expertise_**, it ensures they can get the help they need to meet today's challenges.

4. By providing **_clearer information_** about the benefits available, employers can empower employees to choose the ones that fit their needs.

5. Lastly, when **_enrollment is simplified_**, employees are able to discover the immense value of their benefits. As a result, their appreciation can enhance their loyalty and commitment to their company.

It's understood that having individual one-on-one meetings instead of (or in addition to) a group meeting is not always possible. When travelling or remote employees make up part of your workforce the best practice is to conduct telephone enrollment sessions. It may not be face-to-face, but at least it's still one-on-one. Which is still much more effective than a dreadful group meeting.

How This Process Helps Your Employees

The benefit enrollment counselors work on behalf of your consultant, and know how to position each line of coverage so your employees see the big picture.

What's the big picture you ask? It's whatever matters most to each individual employee.

> *Employees want flexibility, choice and nontraditional options. And they're willing to pay for it. Employees are increasingly willing to bear more of the costs of benefits in order to have a choice of benefits that meet their needs. Especially true among youngest workers who expect customization.*
>
> —MetLife Employee Benefits Trend 2018

From the same study, 60 percent of employees responded positively to the statement:

> *"I am interested in having my employer provide a wider array of non-medical benefits that I can choose to purchase and pay for on my own."*

Conclusion

Many organizations today offer insurance benefits to their people which protect them from unexpected events and provide peace of mind. So why is this difference between Status Quo and NextGeneration open enrollment processes so important? Participation results are on higher and engagement is increased when enrollment is through a tailored and simple shopping experience.

One of the most important things anyone can do for themselves and their families is to be informed on the best available choices offered from their employer's menu of benefit options.

Reshaping the structure of how employees can utilize these programs along with the types of plans offered allows employees to feel acknowledged. Employers can immediately shift to a more human workplace through flexible and personalized benefit programs and communication.

It's not just a win for your most valuable asset (your people), it's also a win for *you*.

CHRIS WOLPERT

Owner & Principal
Group Benefit Solutions
Tacoma, WA

Chris has over ten years of experience in the insurance industry and is the founder of Group Benefit Solutions (GBS). Based in Tacoma, GBS is an employee benefits consulting firm that specializes in helping employers streamline human capital processes with innovative technology solutions, enhance employee engagement with a personalized open enrollment, and create a sustainable healthcare strategy by combining expert specialists with measurable results.

Chris has been interviewed for stories appearing in *U.S. News & World Report, SELF* magazine, Moneyish.com, Clutch.co, *Employee Benefit News,* and *Benefits Pro.*

Chris is originally from Tacoma and received his BA from the Edward R. Murrow School of Communication at Washington State University in Pullman (Go Cougs!). He is the president of the South Puget Sound NAIFA chapter, a member of the South Puget Sound SHRM chapter, and was treasurer of the Kiwanis Club of Steilacoom for four years. Chris's wife, Valerie is the owner of Natural Venom All-Stars, a competitive cheerleading gym in Tacoma that has won two international championships (2012, 2018). They reside in Steilacoom with their three beautiful children, Cara, Carly, and Luke.

gbsbenefitsgroup.com
chris@gbsbenefitsgroup.com
253.228.8336

CHAPTER **NINE**

Miracles Happen But They Don't Come Cheap

The Pros and Cons of Self-Funding Prescription Drug Coverage

KEITH MCNEIL

I magine it's that time of year to renew your health plan. If you are fully-insured you are probably looking at a series of health plan options nicely presented in a colorful spreadsheet. If you are self-funded, the presentation will differ but the analysis of the component parts might focus just on a presentation of stop-loss insurance options (with an equally nice spreadsheet).

In either case, what might not be focused on is the fastest growing cost in a health plan: the rapid increase in drug costs, especially specialty drugs (which are generally considered to be drugs that cost $600 per month or more but can in fact exceed $1,000,000 per year for just one member). One of the reasons for the rapid cost increase is the development of drugs for a very small number individuals who have what are called orphan diseases. The drug manufacturer needs to charge very high costs to try to recoup the cost of developing the drug.

Despite the obvious economic needs of drug manufacturers of drugs for orphan diseases, the pharmaceutical industry has profit margins that are extremely high compared to other industries, and when examining the industry it is clear that many of the manufacturers can be very aggressive in maximizing profits. That can play havoc with health plan costs.

"Miracles happen, gentlemen, but they don't come cheap."

Thus, if you really want to attack the cost of healthcare for your employees, wouldn't it make sense to start with the component that is causing the biggest problem? Before saying yes, understand that the cost of prescription drugs is a complicated area and to maximize the savings requires special expertise.

Prescription drugs costs are already high today and they are expected to only get worse. Experts are predicting that prescription drugs will take a frightening percentage of overall healthcare claims costs in just a few years. Since fully-insured plans control these questions for the members with little or no flexibility (which historically has not solved the cost problem, but see the end of this article), the only alternative is for the plan to be self-funded, including the drug plan. There are pros and cons to self-funding such coverage, and it is important to understand both to optimize this critical facet of healthcare coverage. But first, for groups that are not self-funded already, it is a good idea to determine whether self-funding health coverage even makes sense for a specific employer group.

A fully-insured plan makes all of the rules. It determines which providers are deemed in network, it sets up the plan parameters, it negotiates the approved fee schedules for plan providers, and in the case of prescription drug coverage it selects the Pharmacy Benefit Manager (PBM), it determines the plan's formulary of approved drugs (generally subject to mid-year change without notice), and it keeps any rebates that the drug manufacturers provide. Depending on where the plan sponsor is located, and changing Affordable Care Act (ACA) rules, the surcharge to be fully-insured can be several percent, including state premium taxes—and that is before the insurer's profit margin is added (usually in the three to four percent range, even for non-profit health plans that instead redefine "profit" as an enhancement to reserves). The extra charges and inflexibility of the plan can make self-funding the health insurance, including drug coverage, an attractive option to consider. (As a note to be clear, it is not practical to consider having a fully-insured medical plan but a self-funded drug plan).

The advantages of self-funding the drug coverage are many, but it is important first to consider the two ways that it can be done. One is a "carve-in" and the other is a "carve-out." For our purposes the carve-in generally refers to a bundled medical/Rx plan that is offered by a health plan. This would come under what is called an ASO (Administrative Services Only) agreement. In theory the medical and Rx administration would be seamless, so that the plan would know, for example, how many medical and Rx claims had been paid at any given time (this would be helpful in showing how close the member was to reaching the out-of-pocket limit). In a carve-in model, the plan sponsor does not have a separate, direct contract with the PBM. There is some debate, started by the health plans themselves, that argues the healthcare provided by a bundled carve-in plan is actually better because it provides better and faster information to the treating physician on what drugs the member is using, and this leads to better outcomes. Despite the stridency of such health plan arguments, that would appear to be an unproven allegation at this time.

In a carve-out, the plan sponsor has a direct contract with the PBM, and this is the norm when an independent third-party administrator (TPA) is hired to administer the plan. Depending on the PBM and its ability to transmit data on a daily basis (and the TPA's ability to process that data on a daily basis), the plan sponsor might need to create two separate annual out-of-pocket limits for the member, such as $5,000 for medical care and $1,600 for Rx coverage.

PBMs generally may be broken down into a series of sub-groups. One subgroup is the "big three PBMs" which are: Express Scripts (ESI) (which Cigna has proposed to purchase), Optum Health (owned by United Healthcare), and CVS/Caremark (which is seeking to buy Aetna). The others are all the rest. However, a perhaps more useful line of demarcation is the one that separates "spread pricing" PBMs from "transparent" PBMs, some of whom emphasize that they will act in a fiduciary manner on behalf of the client. The spread pricing contingent, which is especially prevalent with the largest PBMs, makes money by buying the drugs more cheaply than what it charges the plan sponsor. That "spread" is how it makes money. In comparison, the transparent PBMs make money only on the subscription fees that they charge the plan sponsor. While those distinctions are not always black and white, they are accurate enough for our purposes. To put it mildly, the devotees of transparent pricing often have a very low regard for the really big spread-pricing PBMs, with their numerous dubious ways of making money in manners that are anything but transparent. It is not a complete stretch of imagination, perhaps, to liken their view of preparing to work with the large PBMs to the comment made by Obi-Wan Kenobi to Luke Skywalker just before entering the infamous cantina in the first *Star Wars* film: "You will never find a more retched hive of scum and villainy. We must be cautious." OK, that is over the top, but you get the point. The tops PBMs somehow managed to transform a sleepy service business model decades ago into a new model where they became multi-billion dollar behemoths.

One of the big problems with the economic model of the purchase of pharmaceuticals by group health plans is the distorting influence of rebates. Imagine going to McDonald's, ordering a meal, and then after paying a surcharge for it being told that in several months you will get a "rebate" from McDonald's for your purchase to offset the surcharge. You would expect that McDonald's is capable of determining the cost of your meal at the point of purchase instead of surcharging up you front and then sending you a check later to make up for it. In like fashion the drug manufacturer knows the price it is willing to accept for its drug and is fully capable of offering a single net cost up front to the buyer (PBM or direct buyer). So why the rebate, you might ask? The rebate is ultimately a kind of bribe to the PBM in order to influence it in some way, especially in where the drug is positioned in the health plan's drug formulary. If the drug manufacturer knew absolutely that 100 percent of ALL rebates (not just rebates for *some* drugs) were being passed through to the health plan, and thus the PBM had no vested interest in the size of the rebates, the rebate model would serve no purpose. (In a 2017 government hearing with representatives of the pharmaceutical industry, Senator Lamar Alexander asked the obvious question of why rebates even exist, but got no clear answer.) However, it would appear unlikely that any significant change will take place to all of this at the governmental level anytime soon—although the Trump administration has made comments in the direction of reducing or eliminating rebates.

The corrupting influence of rebates is seen for those in a self-funded plan that pay the entire cost of a brand name drug under a high deductible, such as in a Health Savings Account (HSA) plan. The member, let's call him Charley, goes to the pharmacy and pays the full cost of an artificially inflated price. Some months later the employer or plan sponsor receives a payment called a "rebate" but that is really just the overpayment that Charley never knew he made. The fiduciary responsibility of the plan sponsor mandates that the rebate be paid back to Charley, but how often does that happen? The answer is almost never. One PBM has an option where it can accelerate the estimated rebates to the point of sale so that Charley would pay either the exact cost of the drug or a close approximation. Of the PBMs thousands of clients, only *one* has selected this option. (As a side note, the federal government requires employers that receive ACA rebates from their fully-insured carriers for failing to meet their Minimum Loss Ratio mandate to divide up the payment by a pro rata calculation of how much of the total premium each employee paid; thus the precedent is already there.) The PBM industry has a slang term for employers that are not open to sharing the rebates: "rebate addicts." Unfortunately addicts have a way of harming others, in this case Charley.

While the simplicity of the transparent model appeals to many experts and industry pundits, it does not automatically mean that a transparent PBM will have lower net costs; other factors impact the net cost. Leaving aside the actual unit cost of the drug (some larger PBMs might have more clout on pricing than smaller ones, and large PBMs that deal directly with some of the drug manufacturers might see larger rebates than those that work through a rebate aggregator), other decisions made by the health plan can have a major impact on the final net cost. Those include:

- **Generic Fill Rate:** The concept refers to the percentage of drugs purchases that are generic. Generally the higher the percentage the better.

- **Therapeutic Substitution:** This refers to convincing the member and the physician to switch from one drug (usually much more expensive) to a different drug. While often the pharmacist already has the leeway to recommend a generic in lieu of a more expensive brand name drug (so there is no need to contact the prescribing physician), there are other situations that are more complicated and will need the physician's approval.

- **Consumer Education:** This can be the PBM contacting the member by snail mail or electronic means about options to consider that may be better and less costly. It can also include pushing information to the member via a smart phone app (such as the lowest cost pharmacy in the area for a specific drug) or to the pharmacist at point of sale.

- **Tier One Drug Sourcing:** While technically the importation of prescription drugs from outside countries is not legal, the rules are not black and white regarding the importation for personal use only, and the federal government has not pursued legal action against employer groups that allow the purchase from Tier One countries (i.e., Canada, the United Kingdom, Australia, and New Zealand). These countries negotiate directly with the drug manufacturers and thus can have lower cost brand name drugs, including dramatically lower costs in some cases. By importing drugs from these countries, drug costs can be significantly lowered in most cases, and the drugs purchases are identical to the ones that would be purchased in the United States.

- **Drug Manufacturer Coupons:** Many drug companies provide coupons for their brand name drugs, ostensibly to lower the cost of the drug to the consumer. (I say "ostensibly" because the knock on coupons is that they are geared to making the drug cheaper for the member but not the health plan, compared to generic alternatives. Thus a brand name drug priced at $100 but with a $50 coupon would yield an elimination of the member's copay but little help to the health plan, if the cost of a generic is only $10 and the member's copay would pay for that, but since the coupon would pay the member's brand name copay, the member would choose that "free" coverage that would cost the health plan more.) PBMs are now getting smart and coming up with "variable copay" plans that would in that example change the copay to $50, so the health plan would benefit from the coupon if the member chose the brand name over the generic.

- **Patient Assistance Programs:** Drug manufacturers routinely offer patient assistance programs to lower the cost of their drugs for the needy who are uninsured, even to the point of giving them away for free. Some self-funded plans, willing to push the envelope, have taken the stance that the really expensive drugs are not on the formulary and thus are not covered. If a member needs the drugs, the plan would contact the drug manufacturer and say that the member is uninsured and thus see if the drug can be obtained at little or no cost. Patient assistance programs are usually means tested, so they will generally not work for a higher income employee. If the drug manufacturer says no to the request, the health plan then reverts to an unwritten "Plan B" and covers the drug. This is controversial, and if done requires close communication with the stop-loss carrier. (Note: at least one vendor has had success in working with drug manufacturers without having removed the drug from the formulary, so there can be hope here. The same vendor also works with charities and foundations, so it not always necessary to rely solely on the charitable feelings of the drug manufacturers.)

"I think the dosage needs adjusting. I'm not nearly as happy as the people in the ads."

- **Step Therapy:** This requires in some cases the member to try a less expensive drug for efficacy before being allowed a more expensive drug that had been prescribed by the physician.

- **Prior Authorization (PA):** This requires a drug to be pre-authorized by the plan before being dispensed. This is common for specialty drugs and some brand name drugs. There are many reasons why the plan should determine whether a specific expensive drug makes sense compared to lower cost alternatives. This can be a complicated area.

- **Genomic Testing:** Some drugs are designed solely for individuals with specified genetic markers; for others the drug would be useless. Obviously in such cases checking to see if the member had the genetic markers should be step one in the process, but not all health plans are diligent about this surprisingly. I know of a case where a specialist in this area asked a medical office whether it performed genetic testing in all cases for a certain drug. The answer was that the office only did it for Humana patients. When asked why only for Humana insured patients, the answer was that only Humana mandated it. The medical office was unconcerned about the possible large expense of prescribing a drug that was absolutely useless in some cases.

- **Which Drug Costs Are Handled by the PBM?:** A health plan will pay for drugs in a variety of settings, and depending on how the plan is established certain drugs will be handled by the medical portion of the plan (such as drugs administered in the hospital) and the rest will be handled by the PBM. That division is not universal and in general the more the PBM handles the Rx claims of the plan the greater the savings.

- **Narrow Networks or Specialized Formularies:** While most health plans start with the assumption that employees must have access to virtually all pharmacies, with proper data analysis it is possible to create a narrow network of top-named pharmacies that can save a considerable amount of money. The same can be said about tweaking the formulary to be more aggressive in keeping out high priced drugs that have little if any advantage over lower-cost options. The biggest obstacle here is usually direct-to-consumer advertising; the employee that wants a certain drug because he or she saw it advertised on TV (think the "Purple Pill"). Billions of dollars are spent each year because patients asked for the drugs they saw advertised and the doctor complied to avoid having an unhappy patient.

One of the common features of a partially self-funded health plan is the purchase of stop-loss coverage to cover large claims over a certain level. For example, a plan might decide it has the financial resources to cover the first $100,000 of any member's claims per year (with separate aggregate stop-loss protection in case too many claims below $100,000 occur). The plan would purchase coverage to protect against claims over that selected point. It is beyond the scope of this article to explore the intricacies of stop-loss contracts except to say that at least one vendor offers separate coverage just for Rx claims. That would mean there would be a different stop-loss carrier for the medical portion of the plan and the Rx portion. If such a division is considered, special care needs to be taken to make sure the contractual provisions of each plan meet minimum standards (ask, for example, what will happen on renewal if the member has a very large on-going claims, such as hemophilia) and there are no gaps in coverage.

Attacking the growth of prescription drug prices is a necessity for any employer or plan sponsor that is serious about trying to control its health plan spend. The evolving marketplace at the time of the writing of this article has a planned series of mergers of some of the biggest health plans with the biggest PBMs (Cigna, Express Scripts; Aetna, CVS). Will that solve the problem? Will employers have to go through only those health plans to stand a chance of controlling costs? History would appear to say no, but these mergers might have some ability to dampen down increases. For now it appears that only employers on their own, working with an expert consultant, have the ability to optimize the health plan and drug coverage for their employees with a plan that is best suited for them.

KEITH MCNEIL

Partner
Arrow Benefits Group
Petaluma, CA

Keith McNeil, CLU, CEBS, GBDS, began work in 1979 in all aspects of employee benefits brokerage and consulting. He has designations from The American College, and the Wharton School, International Foundation of Employee Benefit Plans.

He is a co-founder of Enwisen, the first web-based employee benefits communication and knowledgebase in the industry; it primarily targeted Fortune 500 companies with a diverse and prestigious client base that included Microsoft, ConAgra, Twentieth Century Fox, and Nissan. (It is now owned by Infor.) He created the Enwisen employee benefits knowledgebase that as early as 1995 provided a web-based communication platform to not only explain at a deep-dive level common medical, dental, and vision plans, but also other sophisticated benefit programs, including 401(k) plans, defined contribution plans, ESOPs, and long term care plans. That program was voted one of the Top Ten new HR programs by Human Resource Executive magazine in 1998.

He has spoken on the pros and cons of self-funding in California and Hawaii and teaches a semi-annual course on COBRA compliance as part of an HR certification course at Santa Rosa Junior College.

arrowbenefitsgroup.com
keithm@arrowbenefitsgroup.com
707.992.3780

CHAPTER TEN

Controlling Healthcare Spend with Reference Based Pricing

What You Should Know . . .

MARCY S. HEATH

We have reached the unfortunate stage where rising health-care costs are eating up the wage gains won by American workers, who are being asked by employers to pick up more of a heftier tab. The average worker is shelling out $5,714 for a family health insurance plan, 30 percent of the total $17,764 cost. Five years ago, workers shouldered $4,316 of the $15,745 cost, or 27 percent.

Over the past five years, premiums for an employer provided family insurance plan have climbed 19 percent, while worker pay increased 12 percent. The U.S. Labor Department's Consumer Price Index climbed 6 percent over the past five years.

Deductibles, or preset amounts an insured employee must spend before their major medical coverage can begin, are now an increasingly routine feature of employer provided plans. Eighty-one percent of workers now face a deductible, up from 72 percent in 2012, at an average $1,505 for a single employee, up from $1,097 in 2012. About one in ten workers has a current deductible of $3,000, if not higher.

The United States spends about 18 percent of its gross domestic product on healthcare, nearly twice as much as most other developed countries. The Congressional Budget Office has said that if medical cost continues to grow unabated, "total spending on health care would eventually account for all of the country's economic output."

Pulling Back the Healthcare Provider's Curtain

Hospitals, drug companies, device makers, physicians, and other providers can benefit by charging inflated prices, favoring the costliest treatment options, and curbing competition that could give patients more affordable options. Almost every interaction is an opportunity to send multiple, often opaque bills with a long list of charges.

A major factor behind the high cost is that the United States does not regulate or intervene in medical pricing, aside from setting payment rates for Medicare and Medicaid. Many other countries deliver health care on a private fee-for-service basis, as does much of the American healthcare system, but they set rates for health care by negotiating with providers and insurers nationwide. Such systems wield much greater control over what kind of medical procedures, medications, and therapies are available to consumers. They conduct cost-effectiveness reviews to decide if a service is worth the investment of limited healthcare dollars. The United States has resisted all attempts to adopt a similar approach.

A 2012 report from the Institute of Medicine estimated that the United States health system wastes about $750 billion annually. Unnecessary services make up the largest category of waste. Other segments were excess administrative cost and an overabundance of efforts to document care given to patients.

Until the last decade, colonoscopies were mostly performed in a physician's office on patients with high risk for colon cancer, or to seek a diagnosis for intestinal bleeding. Several studies by gastroenterologists found that a colonoscopy detected early cancers and precancerous growths in otherwise healthy people. However, they did not compare screening colonoscopies with far less invasive and cheaper screening methods, including an annual test for blood in the stool or a sigmoidoscopy, which screens the lower colon where most cancers occur.

The increased volume of colonoscopies rose 50 percent from 2003 to 2009 for consumers with commercial insurance. If the American healthcare system were a true market, the increased volume might have brought down the cost because of the economies of scale and more competition, instead, it became a new business opportunity.

Although many procedures can be performed in a physician's office or in a separate surgery center, prices skyrocket at the special centers, as do profits. Insurers pay an additional "facility fee" to ambulatory surgery centers and hospitals that is intended to cover their higher costs. When popularized in the 1980s, outpatient surgical centers were addressed as a cost-saving option, as they cut down on expensive hospital stays for minor operations. Cost savings have been offset as procedures once performed in a physician setting have filled up the centers and bills have multiplied.

In 2009, the last year for which statistics are available, gastroenterologists performed more procedures in ambulatory surgery centers than specialists of any other field. Once they bought into a center, the number of procedures performed rose 27 percent. The specialists earned an average of $433,000 a year, among the highest-paid doctors.

Consider This

Consumers do not see prices until after a service is provided, if they see them at all. This is the normal practice of your traditional "network" attached to your current health plan. There is little quality data on hospitals and doctors to assist consumers in determining good value, aside from surveys conducted by websites and magazines. Consumers with insurance pay a fraction of the bill, providing minimal disincentive for spending.

Physicians often do not know the cost of the test and procedures they recommend to their patients. Payments are determined in countless negotiations between the physician, hospital, pharmacy, and an insurer, with the result often depending on their relative negotiating power. Insurers have limited incentive to bargain forcefully since they can raise your premiums to cover the cost.

Some large employers have begun fighting back on cost. Safeway realized they were paying between $848 and $5,984 for a colonoscopy in California. The company established an all inclusive "reference price" they were willing to pay, which was set at a level high enough to allow employees access a range of high quality options. Above that price, employees were required to pay the difference. Safeway chose $1,250 and found plenty of providers willing to accept the price.

Introducing Reference Based Pricing

As you try to endure increases related to healthcare cost, employers often contemplate different plan designs and what will produce the most significant cost savings. Employers consider Preferred Provider Organization plans (PPOs) as an option and are hopeful that incorporating one with their plan will be a winning solution as claim charges will appear better on paper once network discounts are applied. The problem, as laid out above, is care costs continue to rise at an unprecedented pace. The PPO discounts are not enough to offset the extreme pricing inflation. When providers, facilities, and other healthcare services do not share their "true cost," a discount is a moot approach to implement as a strategy to control cost. What price exactly are you getting a discount off? The insurance network has been the cornerstone of many insurance carriers' value propositions.

But referenced based pricing plans do not make use of network contracts. Many self-funded plans see less value in obtaining "network agreements."

Hospitals and facilities with market power are more likely to rely on chargemasters as a reimbursement tool. Since Medicare changed its hospital reimbursement formula to the prospective payment system in 1985, the chargemaster—a list of billable items and prices for all services provided to patients—has diminished in the importance in determining Medicare reimbursement.

It is still used in determining Medicare outlier payments; those are the extra payments for cases involving high cost. Commercial insurers pay hospitals based on either diagnosis related groups, per diem, or the discounted chargemaster price. Most public and commercial insurers do not pay hospitals their full chargemaster prices. In the early '80s, the chargemaster charges would cost 10 percent above the listed chargemaster price. Today, the inflated charges are as much as 2850 percent above the set rate. What good is your PPO discount if the charges are inflated? The larger inflated charges are found in the Southeast, Georgia is currently charging 737 percent while Florida is at 901 percent.

In the quest to decrease the employee healthcare spend, some employers are implementing a revolutionary concept called Reference Based Pricing. Reference Based Pricing is a system used for cost containment purposes.

Reference Based Pricing refers to prices that are not tied to traditional insurance carrier or rented network that negotiates discounts from provider billed charges. The traditional discount results in the allowed amount the health plan pays the provider. This groundbreaking concept sets provider reimbursement on a percentage of what Medicare would pay the provider. Pricing typically ranges from 120 percent to 150 percent above Medicare.

Reference Based Pricing (RBP) has been tested and has produced significant savings for employers who have implemented this cost containment strategy. As discussed earlier, Safeway saved $700,000 in 2008, the first year it implemented RBP to curb prescription drug cost. The grocery store chain saved an additional $2.7 million in 2009 as it expanded its RBP program to also include labs and certain common diagnostic procedures, such as colonoscopies.

The California Public Employees' Retirement System (CalPERS) targeted joint replacements with its RPB strategy, saving $2.6 million from their medical spend and another $5.5 million in 2012.

How Reference Based Pricing Works

Cardiologists use echocardiograms to diagnose heart value problems. The hospital may bill $3500 for the echocardiogram. The insurance network may have negotiated a 40 percent discount, so the allowed amount is $2100. This is the amount that is billed to your medical plan. Depending on how much of the deductible and co-insurance has been satisfied by the employee will determine how the charges are distributed. For example, if your plan has a $3000 major medical deductible and your employee has not satisfied any portion of that deductible, the total charge will be applied to the deductible. The employee will be responsible for the full bill.

With RBP, Medicare often pays about $150 for an echocardiogram. If the RBP is set at 150 percent of Medicare, the health plan would pay $225 regardless if the procedure was performed in the hospital or physician's office. From the example above, if your plan has a $3000 major medical deductible and you had RBP, the employee would only be charged $225 if they have not already satisfied their deductible.

The Goal of Reference Based Pricing and Indirect Ways of Lowering Cost

The goal of reference-based pricing is to reduce an employer's healthcare spend. This can be accomplished in several ways, the most common is by setting a procedure's price point lower than the normal allowed amount. This results in direct savings to the plan sponsor (employer) while allowing the plan sponsor to control future cost trend. Future costs may be controlled by either directing how much to increase the reference point when renewing, or by attaching to Medicare, which historically had cost reimbursement increases that were lower than overall commercial medical trend. Estimates put reference-based pricing savings between five percent and 15 percent for a full implementation. Most savings are a result of claims from non-emergency facilities where typical allowed charges are often double, or higher, than they are under Medicare. In contrast, physician claims are normally around 130 percent of Medicare, and are not a significant source of savings for most reference-based pricing arrangements. If implemented on a limited set of procedures, reference-based price savings are typically much smaller, often in the low single digits.

Reference Based Pricing brings some indirect assistance in lowering cost:

- Implementing reference-based pricing requires an understanding of how multiple procedures under one claim incident are priced. It also provides plan sponsors a better understanding of what is being billed. Transparency brings opportunities to discover billing errors and eliminate wasteful spending.
- Putting pressure on healthcare providers may eventually assist in lowering market prices. In the CalPERS example, the employer was large enough to have negotiation leverage. Hospitals didn't want to lose their business, so they accepted a 34 percent decline in prices charged for specific procedures at higher priced facilities.
- Engaged employees are more likely to compare prices and make informed healthcare decisions. When implementing a reference based pricing plan, educating employees about healthcare cost and encouraging them to be proactive with their health care decisions is imperative. This communication needs to take place several times with employees during the first year of implementing reference-based pricing.

Traditional Insurers Have Adopted Referenced Based Pricing

The nation's second-largest insurer began offering employers a coverage plan for their workers which include set prices for certain medical procedures. While Reference Based Pricing has been catching on, what's different is WellPoint offers set prices for roughly 900 medical services. WellPoint offers regional limits on specific medical services. Employees who choose to spend more than the reference amount are required to pay the difference. WellPoint offers employers the option to rebate the cost of a procedure, if an employee selects a service provider that performs a procedure at a price below the reference point.

National General introduced an option for employers, a plan including referenced based pricing, called Core Value. This plan design, combined with other benefits of their self-funded program, offers employees the same quality of care and benefits, while maintaining a less costly and predictable payment. There are no networks associated with the plan, so plan members have the freedom to use any provider they choose. However, some services still rely on the use of network providers such as pharmacy benefits and transplants.

Reference Based Pricing Limitations Under the Affordable Care Act

The Affordable Care Act (ACA) imposes limitations on the structure of reference-based plans. Failure to follow these guidelines will result in amounts paid by patients above the reference price,

HERE'S HOW CORE VALUE PAYS BENEFITS

Core Value pays for the following rates for covered services:

- **Doctor Office Visits:** 130% of the Medicare reimbursement rate[*]
- **Inpatient Services:** 150% of the Medicare reimbursement rate[*]
- **Outpatient Services:** 130% of the Medicare reimbursement rate[*]
- **Dialysis:** 100% of the Medicare

Benefit Example

Not an actual case, presented for illustrative purposes only.

Billed charge for covered services	$3,376
Medicare reimbursement rate	$1,571
Plan Maximum Allowable Amount (MAA)	$2,043 [1,2]
Member Coinsurance Responsibility (80/20)	$409
Plan pays:	**$1,634**

[*] Or other derived equivalent

[1] 130% of the Medicare reimbursement rate

[2] Sometimes members may be Balanced Billed for the amounts in excess of the plan MAA. This is where the Member Advocacy Program can help to negotiate an agreed upon amount with the provider.

SOURCE: National General Benefits Solutions. *Lower Your Health Benefit Costs with Core Value.* PDF. Arlington, TX: National Health Insurance Company, September 2017. https://www.ngicbenefits.com/NGBS-COREVALUEINSERT.09.14.17_download.pdf.

counting toward the patient's out-of-pocket maximum. For 2018, the limit has been set at $7,350 for an individual and $14,700 for family. This would effectively cap potential plan savings by placing the balance bill back on the plan sponsor, and removing incentives for the patient to choose quality, cost effective, and compliant providers. The following are structure limitations provided by the U. S. Department of Labor:

- **Adequacy:** Plans should have procedures in place to ensure they are maintaining an adequate number of providers that will accept the reference price. This can be open to interpretation, however, plans are encouraged to consider network-adequacy approaches developed by states, as well as reasonable geographic distance measures. In addition, patient wait times must be reasonable.

- **Time:** Plans are required to offer the member sufficient time to make a choice of a provider once the need for care has been established. Because of this provision, reference-based pricing cannot apply to emergency care.

- **Exceptions:** This should be easily accessible, and services rendered by providers that do not accept the reference price should be treated by the plan as if they were administered by a provider that did accept the reference price if: (a) access is unavailable to a provider that accepts the reference price, or, (b) quality could be compromised with the reference price provider.

- **Disclosure:** A fee may not be charged for the following disclosures: (a) information on pricing structure, which should be provided automatically; and (b) upon request, a list of providers accepting the reference price, a list of providers accepting a negotiated price above the reference price, and information on the process and underlying data that ensure quality standards are met by the providers accepting the reference price.

Reference Based Pricing May Help Employers Avoid the ACA Excise Tax (a.k.a., "Cadillac Tax")

On January 22, 2018, Congress passed, and the President signed into effect, a two-year delay of the 40 percent excise tax on high-cost employer sponsored health plans, also known as the "Cadillac Tax." No regulations have been issued to date. In February and July 2015, the Internal Revenue Service (IRS) issued notices covering several issues concerning the Cadillac Tax, and requested comments on the possible approaches that could ultimately be incorporated into proposed regulations. While the tax was originally non-tax deductible, December 2015 changes made it tax deductible for employers who pay it.

The permanent, annual tax on high-cost employer sponsored health coverage will be implemented beginning in 2022. The purpose of the tax is to help finance the expansion of health coverage under the Affordable Care Act (ACA), reduce excess health care spending by employees and employers, and reduce tax preferred treatment of employer provided healthcare.

The tax is 40 percent of the cost of health coverage that exceeds predetermined threshold amounts. Cost includes the total contributions paid by both the employer and employees, but not cost-sharing amounts such as deductibles, co-insurance, or copays when care is received.

Employers may implement reference-based pricing strategies to help limit excessive provider payments and costs. The strategies are proven to save 20 percent, or more for targeted procedures, without compromising access to quality providers.

Implement Reference Based Pricing with Success

Reference-based pricing is generally structured one of three ways, *Most Common*, *Mid-Level*, or *Full Implementation*. Employers need to decide what level of Reference Based Pricing they want to establish. Would you want to apply RBP to specific procedures like the CalPERS plan? Do you want to cover the entire spectrum? Or do you wish to be somewhere in between?

Let's review the structures provided:

Most Common

Reference prices only reference certain procedures such as knee and hip replacement, colonoscopies, or MRIs. These procedures are chosen because they have uniform protocols, making price comparisons easier. Implement a concierge service bundled with medical management. A concierge service improves the predictability of great healthcare. Statistics prove the top reasons employees call medical concierge service:

EMPLOYEES CALL CONCIERGE FOR...

⊕	Medical/Surgical Referral	43%
⊕	Medical Coaching	23%
⊕	Primary Care	12%
⊕	Imaging/Diagnostic	9%
⊕	Medical Review	7%
⊕	Mental Health	4%
⊕	Second Opinions	2%

SOURCE: "What The Health Insurance Companies Don't Want You To Know." WellNet Healthcare: John Augustine. WellNet.com. March 14, 2018. Accessed September 18, 2018. https://wellnet.com/broker-resource/marketing/what-the-health-insurance-companies-dont-want-you-to-know/.

By implementing concierge bundled with medical management, you are coaching employees to utilize medical management which is *essential* to a successful RBP plan. You are planting the seed to *Full Implementation* of an RBP plan. At the end of the plan year, you will obtain data from your medical management that should help you make an informed decision as to your next steps.

Mid-Level Implementation

Reference pricing is utilized for all out-of-network claims. This means the reference pricing essentially replaces the "usual and customary" pricing that is typically in place.

Employers may choose to build in a PPO network for PCP/specialist visits, and RBP the hospital and ancillary charges. As Safeway has proven, small steps implemented can still produce significant savings. The grocery store chain implemented reference-based pricing the first year to curb prescription drug cost. The second year, Safeway expanded its Reference Based Pricing program to also include labs and certain common diagnostic procedures, such as colonoscopies. Employers have the option to choose a specific procedure or benefit option thanks to RBP.

I advise clients to implement concierge and medical management services, as it is vital to the success of your benefits plan.

Full Implementation

Full implementation includes reference pricing on almost all billed claims, except for emergency care and sometimes physician services.

*Emergency care is not included, so as not to fall afoul of ACA rules.

I advise clients to implement concierge and medical management services, as it is vital to the success of your benefits plan.

Employee Communication

Reference-based pricing cannot be successful unless you have 100-percent employee understanding and participation. When RBP is first introduced, employees often assume that it will limit them to an approved list of providers and facilities. Employee skepticism and confusion can cause them to throw up their guard. There is a whole education process employers and employees need to go through to make sure the strategic implementation isn't upset by the members reaction. The RBP model breaks with what consumers are used to, and for that matter, hospitals will probably send a bill for an amount beyond the negotiated service price in hopes of collecting from the consumer. It's the job of the RBP service provider to resolve the issue, but the job of the employee to send the *EOB* (Explanation of Benefits). Communication needs to be very clear and should take place more than once during the plan year. Employees have guided support from medical management and concierge staff, therefore it is imperative to introduce your members to this service prior to full implementation. Having this great service for your employees reduces friction and makes for an easy transition to reference-based pricing.

In a recent study by George Loewenstein from Carnegie Mellon University, he found that only 14 percent of employees could answer basic questions on insurance features. Employees need ongoing guidance for insurance and it's especially true for those on RBP plans. The only way for RBP to succeed is through patient advocacy and education.

Education and Communication is Key to a Successful RBP!

MARCY S. HEATH

President
Inoventive Solutions
Bremen, GA

Marcy S. Heath is President and founder of Inoventive Solutions. She has over 20 years' experience advising clients with innovative benefit solutions. Having worked with well over 200 employer clients, representing several thousand individuals, Marcy has gained a rich insight that allows her to provide proactive solutions that create successful outcomes for employers and employees. Marcy has been proactive in the pursuit to change how employers manage their healthcare supply chain while improving employee benefits and increasing bottom line profits for employers.

With a consultative approach and implementing innovative solutions, Marcy is successful with assisting employers in slashing their medical spend. Our most recent client saved $195,000 annually by implementing cost containment strategies provided by Inoventive Solutions.

An established industry thought leader and certified health care reform specialist, Marcy has been a featured speaker on several different platforms, providing valuable insight into ACA law, rules guidelines and compliance within the law.

Marcy is a member of the NextGeneration Benefits Mastermind Partnership—an elite national network of strategic, forward thinking business consultants and benefit advisors.

www.inoventivesolutions.us
marcy@inoventivesolutions.us
678.215.4634

CHAPTER ELEVEN

Credit Unions . . . Breaking the Healthcare Bank

JOHN HARRIS

The Law of Large Numbers

C redit unions are often considered innovators in the financial services world. Even though they only hold about eight percent of the U.S. banked population total assets, the credit union community is filled with great thought leaders, unafraid of challenging the status quo. They are also known to be one of the most collaborative industry groups, sharing knowledge and joining forces with their peers to create strength and economies of scale.

When it comes to employee benefits, a group of credit union leaders have figured out how to replace the broken healthcare system with a model that allows them to purchase benefits like Costco or Walmart. Most employers have been purchasing benefits the same way for years. Those old strategies don't work in a healthcare system that has changed dramatically in the past decade. The cost of healthcare has grossly outpaced wages and inflation. The average annual premium for family medical coverage has increased a staggering 191 percent over the past twenty years. Something has to give.

The Day of Reckoning

On a grey, drizzly day in a Pacific Northwest Credit Union boardroom, a small group of credit union executives asked the $64,000 question, "Is there a better way to manage our employee healthcare expense?" The result of this initial meeting was the prelude of what would become a major shift in how credit unions and other similar employer groups figured out how to change the employee benefits buying model and take control away from the big insurance carriers. It became clear, very quickly, that the insurance company is not incented to lower an employer's healthcare cost. All you have to do is answer one simple question, "Who does the insurance company work for?" The response is always the same—SHAREHOLDERS.

The following graph illustrates how well insurance companies have been performing for their shareholders:[1]

---

[1] SOURCE: "Stock Summary." Stock Profile. Ameritrade.com. https://research.tdameritrade.com/grid/public/research/stocks/summary.

	Share Price June 2010	Share Price June 2018	Share Price Increase
Aetna	$27.28	$191.81	603%
Anthem/Blue Cross	$48.05	$250.51	421%
Cigna	$31.94	$182.10	470%
United Healthcare	$27.07	$251.43	829%

These are stellar returns!

If you don't believe it, just compare them to some of America's top performing blue chip companies:[2]

	Share Price June 2010	Share Price June 2018	Share Price Increase
Johnson & Johnson	$56.53	$124.24	120%
McDonalds	$65.88	$162.79	147%
Microsoft	$24.02	$101.41	322%
Walmart	$47.57	$84.31	77%

Rather than dive into all the reasons why health insurance company stocks are outperforming many of the best companies in the U.S., just make note that they are. Then remember, it can't be happening because they are lowering the cost of insurance to their customers.

---

[2] SOURCE: "Stock Summary." Stock Profile. Ameritrade.com. https:// research.tdameritrade.com/grid/public/research/stocks/summary.

Get Educated

Like most employers, credit union leaders have been educated (brainwashed), by the insurance industry, to believe there was nothing they could do about their annual six to 10 percent rate increases. So, the C-Suite often kicked the can to the HR department to 'manage' their third largest expense. This action resulted in allowing HR managers to have P&L responsibility that was misaligned with their expertise. HR managers generally have a skill set for managing recruitment, hiring, compensation, benefits administration, training, legal compliance, discipline, and employment termination. Although, managing how employee benefits are administered within the organization is one of their roles, being accountable for engineering a financially sustainable strategy is not. That function is mostly relegated to their broker, whose financial interest is often aligned with their insurance carrier partners.

The first thing this group of credit union executives had to do was embrace the fact that a paradigm shift was required. They couldn't continue doing the same things they had been doing and expect results to magically get better. They had to deconstruct the entire health benefits buying process and rebuild it in a way that gave them control of the healthcare supply chain. In order to do this, they needed to get educated on how the healthcare system worked. It's the same process they might go through when evaluating options to improve their ROA or CAMEL (Capital, Asset Quality, Management, Earnings, Asset/Liability Management) rating. As with those initiatives, it's not easy. But, it's necessary to be a high performer.

Understanding how insurance works and how the cost is determined can be very complicated. But, one fact is constant in group health insurance. The larger the number of employees covered in a group, the lower the cost per employee. Also, having a larger number of employees, reduces the potential for excessive risk (claims exceeding premium paid). It's the law of large numbers principle. The same reason Walmart can sell product for less than the local hardware store is because they buy in huge volume and get a lower cost per item. This simple concept sparked a revolution for these credit union executives.

See the chart below, illustrating the law of large numbers and showing how the probability of having a "bad" claims year diminishes as the number of employees in the group increase. A "bad" claims year occurs when claims exceed 125 percent of the expected claims according to an insurance underwriter.

The "Ah Ha" Moment

Armed with the law of large numbers principle, the next step was to determine exactly what is considered a large enough number of employees. Is it 500 employees? Is it 5,000 employees? From a group medical underwriting perspective, a statistically large number would be something greater than 1,000 covered employees. But, there's a *small* problem; 98 percent of all credit unions have less than 1,000 employees. How could they possibly create the law of large numbers when their individual credit union only has 50 or 100 or 200 employees? There is only one answer. Join multiple credit unions together as a single, large purchaser. But, that can't be done . . . can it?

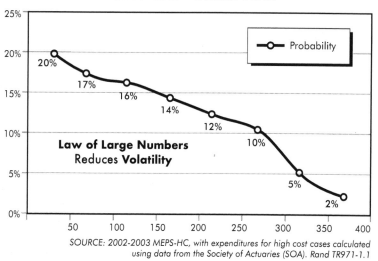

PURCHASES AS A LARGE GROUP, PROBABILITY OF A "BAD" CLAIMS YEAR

SOURCE: 2002-2003 MEPS-HC, with expenditures for high cost cases calculated using data from the Society of Actuaries (SOA). Rand TR971-1.1

The idea of aggregation is not a new concept. However, it is challenging when you are talking about bringing disparate employers together while maintaining ERISA and DOL compliance. Employee benefits are highly regulated, and the fact that most organizations want to offer different plan designs, different provider networks, and different employee contribution levels, make aggregating employers together for the purpose of buying healthcare, similar to herding cats!

But, if we use the keep it simple principle, enlightenment happens. Who said you had to become one large group to *buy* like a large group? By deconstructing the entire healthcare purchasing model, these credit union executives were able to maintain all the individualism they needed while leveraging the power of aggregating risk with other credit unions.

The Blueprint

This group of bright executives began outlining something that would change the status quo and create a paradigm shift for credit unions. A secret that few will discover.

- **Step 1:** Determine the largest components of the healthcare spend
- **Step 2:** Work on reducing the top three healthcare cost drivers
- **Step 3:** Share the knowledge with other credit unions

Step 1: Determine The Largest Components of Healthcare Spend

The components of group healthcare cost can be divided into two buckets: Fixed costs and Variable costs. Fixed costs (15-20% of total cost) cover plan administration, claims administration, stop-loss insurance, broker fees, and insurance carrier profits. Variable cost (80-85% of total cost) cover medical claims. After dissecting every piece of the group healthcare puzzle, the executives determined the following top three factors dictate the price they pay for healthcare for their organizations:

- Severity and frequency of claims paid per employee per year (variable cost)
- Healthcare provider and facility selection (variable cost)
- Stop-loss insurance (fixed cost)

Step 2: Work on Reducing the Top Three Healthcare Cost Drivers

Since claims make up the majority of the group health spend, it seems to be the logical place to begin. Just following good math principles, work on reducing the largest number first. An interesting thing these credit union executives found was that all three of the top healthcare cost drivers worked together and affected the outcome of the others.

For example, if an employee selected one provider over another, the claims cost was different. If one provider offered alternative treatment, the claims cost was different. If the individual stop-loss limit was increased, the cost went down and the employer had an incentive to steer employees to high quality and better value providers.

The first thing the executives decided to do was find the best medical management resource team that would come alongside their employees and hand-hold them through both the health delivery and health plan (aka "insurance") systems. They knew that a higher touch and deeper dive concierge model of service would create better employee healthcare choices. They wanted to make sure that employees were getting the right care, in the right time, at the right place, and for the right price. This was critical to reducing the severity and frequency of claims.

The second thing was to address the largest fixed cost component, stop-loss insurance. Stop-loss insurance is a policy designed to limit claim losses to a specific amount. This type of coverage is to ensure that catastrophic claims (specific stop-loss) or numerous claims (aggregate stop-loss), do not upset the financial reserves of a health plan. Stop-loss insurance exists in both fully-insured plans and self-funded plans. However, an employer has no control over the stop-loss provided in a fully-insured plan because it is only the insurance carrier that is affected by the make up and results of the policy. In a self-funded plan, the employer can purchase stop-loss insurance in a manner consistent with its goals rather than an insurance company's goals.

Step 3: Share the Knowledge with Other Credit Unions

The credit union executives figured out that the cost and risk, associated with their stop-loss coverage, shrank as the number of covered employees in their plan increased. This goes back to the law of large numbers principle. So, they devised a way to bring multiple credit union employers together for the purpose of aggregating risk and purchasing stop-loss insurance.

They called it the Credit Union Healthcare Coalition. The basic premise of the program is to allow each credit union to pool their employees together and purchase a single stop-loss insurance policy for the entire group. Rather than paying the higher price as a small employer, they were able to get bulk pricing as a very large employer. And, they were able to mitigate risk to each individual credit union. The more credit unions that join the coalition, the lower the net cost to each.

Sounds good but does it work?

Unfortunately, most employers have accepted the status quo and believe if their renewal comes in below healthcare inflation trend, they are getting a good deal. They are budgeting for six to 10 percent increases annually. But, for those who have taken

HISTORICAL COST PER EMPLOYEE PER YEAR
FOR MEDICAL/VISION/RX

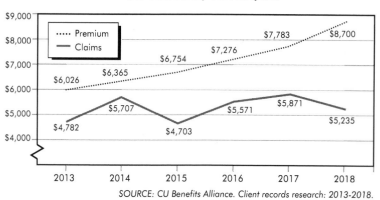

SOURCE: CU Benefits Alliance. Client records research: 2013-2018.

the time and effort, like this group of credit union executives, the results have been amazing. The graph below illustrates one of the credit union's results after implementing the strategies outlined in this chapter. The bottom graphical line shows what the group actually paid each year. The top line shows what they would have paid, had they continued using the old status quo ideology. This particular group had 155 employees and generated over $1 million in cost reduction over five years.

Conclusion

Where do you take your employee benefits strategy from here? You only have two choices; remain in the status quo and keep getting the same rate increase year after year or take the new road, the next generation in healthcare. If you select option one, you should probably invest in health insurance company stocks because they will continue delivering a superior return to shareholders. Choose wisely.

JOHN HARRIS

CEO
CU Benefits Alliance
Plano, TX

John Harris is the CEO and co-founder of CU Benefits Alliance. John is a performance-driven leader with cross-functional expertise in insurance, marketing, strategic planning, operations, data analytics, business development and agency management. He is a leading authority on credit union healthcare coalitions and collaborations.

CU Benefits Alliance is an employee benefits consulting firm whose mission is to help credit unions build their own NextGen Benefits architecture. CU Benefits has been recognized by the National Association of Credit Union Service Organizations (NACUSO) as its Credit Union Service Organization of the Year, for excellence and innovation in use of the collaborative model to help credit unions better manage employee benefits.

www.cuBenefitsAlliance.com
jharris@cuBenefitsAlliance.com
877.674.7555

CHAPTER TWELVE

Leveraging Your Buying Power Through Association Membership

How Small-to-Medium-Size Businesses Can Buy Employee Benefits like Larger Businesses by Leveraging the Buying Power of Professional Associations

TOM DORYWALSKI & TREY TAYLOR

A professional association is an organization formed to unite and inform people who work in the same occupation or business community. There are many advantages to joining such associations from professional networking, to educational opportunities, the ability to influence political policy, and consolidate purchasing power for strategic assets and services. These associations exist in every state in the country.

Professional associations exist to bring disparate benefits to their membership that would otherwise be impossible or difficult to obtain elsewhere. Many association members who lead busy professional lives depend on their association to brief them on important industry trends, new legislative rulings, and advances in technology. While these associations may have started as a way to build solidarity or standardize access to information, economic and business benefits have been added to the list of reasons to maintain a membership in such an organization.

In recent years, healthcare costs have emerged as one of the primary challenges to growth in American business. These costs drive down profitability, divert necessary resources from growth-producing activities, complicate recruiting and retention measures, and introduce complexity into daily business activities. Unfortunately, the sizable investments required from businesses have not translated into a stable, viable employee benefit producing superior health outcomes. Rather, small businesses have seen annual compound premium growth in the double digits and have been forced to respond in ways that have restricted their employees' access to healthcare. To many businesses, the benefit has become a detriment.

It's not only businesses that suffer. Rising health-care costs are eating up the increased wages of American workers who are being asked by their employers to share in the increased cost of benefits. In 2012 the average worker spent 27 percent of take-home pay on health insurance costs, now that number exceeds 33 percent according to the Kaiser Family Foundation. In fact, the burden of funding health coverage at work has increased faster than both wage growth and inflation for many years leaving workers increasingly behind and household budgets increasingly under pressure.

In response to the prevailing situation, the Trump administration issued Executive Order 13813 which sought to facilitate the "adoption and administration" of association-based health plans to "expand access to affordable health coverage for employees of small employers and certain self-employed individuals." The final regulations promulgated in response to this Executive Order read:

"By participating in [association-based health plans], employees of small employers and working owners are able to obtain coverage that is not subject to the regulatory complexity and burden that currently characterizes the market for individual and small group health coverage and, therefore, can enjoy flexibility with respect to benefit package design comparable to that enjoyed by large employers."

The momentum for these plans has begun. Touting the advantages of association-based plans, U.S. Secretary of Labor, Alexander Acosta stated, *"Many of our laws, particularly Obamacare, make health care coverage more expensive for small businesses than large companies, [Association plans] are about more choice, more access, and more coverage."* The Congressional Budget Office, a non-partisan agency that provides the U.S. Congress with budget estimates, projects that over 4 million people will obtain their health insurance through an association-based health plan by 2023.

The subject legislation specifically removes undue restrictions on establishing and implementing association-based health plans by eliminating prior legal proscriptions, recasting definitions, and expanding the number of associations eligible for more flexible underwriting and plan design rules that previously were available only to larger employer groups. Associations can now sponsor plans that bring the benefits of combined purchasing power to small businesses. Whether an association-based plan is constructed under these regulations as an Association Health Plan (AHP), or whether they are constructed more of an affinity group purchasing contract, the benefits to associations and members are largely the same.

Small business members of Professional Associations face many challenges in today's marketplace, the most daunting of which is their ability to effectively compete with larger companies. All too often the limited financial resources of a small business create competitive disadvantages that negatively affect production capacity, technological innovation, sales distribution, marketing and the recruitment and retention of talented employees. When added to these challenges, the soaring costs of healthcare pose an existential threat.

In discussions with their members, associations around the country have recognized this fact and the more proactive among them are implementing association-based health plans to benefit their members, and in so doing are making great strides towards solving this complex problem. Initial results show that approximately 40 percent of employers joining these plans have never offered benefits before. Instead their employees were uninsured or were required to purchase Obamacare plans. With group plans these employees are seeing the total cost of ownership of health insurance decrease.

Of course, bringing employers together to buy health insurance is not a novel concept—the idea has been around for decades. Historically, the fully-insured carriers have provided phantom premium discounts to members of certain associations to simplify the sales channel. Unfortunately, the economics of these plans are no different from any other block of fully-insured business and soon the spiral double-digit premium increases, lack of claims transparency, fiduciary misalignment and cost-shifting begins. These factors lead the quality plan participants to seek other alternatives which acknowledge their lower Medical Loss Ratios and plan utilization and they leave the plan which is left with only high utilization and unprofitable companies as members. The curse of adverse selection in the fully-insured market leads to the all-too-common death spiral and the plan itself implodes under the weight of its own usage.

It is only self-insured plans that provide the high level of flexibility necessary to introduce next-generation cost-saving concepts and increased benefit levels necessary for success. Plans that are allowed to avail themselves of products and services which serve to manage the Healthcare Value Chain produce superior performance for their members—whether in or out of an association framework. For example, the ability to identify and evacuate unnecessary claims dollars from the plan using techniques such as international prescription sourcing, tax advantaged wellness, medically managing claims, or even advanced HRA strategies—these strategies are most effective on a self-insured platform.

When a fully-insured carrier is present, it has a fiduciary duty to its shareholders to siphon off the profits of the plan for the benefit of the insurance company as a whole. With self-insured plans, those same profits are used to fund claims and the costs of innovative strategies. The former causes the death spiral; the latter avoids it. Association-based plans must be on a self-insured platform to ensure longevity, flexibility and utility. Members are well-advised to confirm the nature of the plan (self-insured vs. fully-insured) while investigating the association-based plan as a potential solution.

Those associations that have implemented an association-based plan have identified three primary drivers for their decision to offer a plan to their members:

The first decision driver is price. Establishing an association-based plan allows individual employers who are Members of the Association to benefit from the combination of the group's purchasing power. The old saying goes that there's power in numbers. This is clearly the case with association-based plans which bring together businesses and use their collective buying power to get lower premiums on the insurance products they purchase. Many businesses already do this when they buy other items like paper goods and office supplies, and more and more businesses are turning to a group purchasing approach to reduce health insurance costs, as well.

Typically, association-based health plans deliver an upfront premium savings of up to 30 percent over comparably designed plans in the marketplace. Additionally, when properly managed, these plans offer annual renewal rates of less than 5 percent, as opposed to the average 22 percent for small group plans in the market. If an association-based plan doesn't provide substantial savings upfront for its members and a low renewal rate increase, it isn't serving its purpose.

The second decision driver is choice. Every dollar matters, of course, and lower premium prices are a clear benefit of group purchasing participation in association-based health plans, but it's imperative that Association Members be able to purchase a health plan capable of meeting their own individual needs and not a "one-size-fits-all" plan. This requirement will reveal itself in flexible plan design options, but also in special underwriting concessions so that every employee can be covered. The typical association-based health plan has allows Members to customize deductibles, coinsurance, copays, and pharmacy benefits. If an association-based plan doesn't provide preferred underwriting and substantial plan design flexibility, it hasn't been implemented correctly.

The third decision driver is satisfaction. For an association-based health plan to be successful it must satisfy the needs of each of its stakeholders. The most effective means to measure true satisfaction with a health plan is to gauge annual plan renewal rates—how many employers opt to continue offering the plan for the following year. If a plan delivers lower upfront premium costs and aggressive renewal increases, high plan design flexibility and broad underwriting, the number of employers renewing the plan will be very high. If a plan fails in these measures, renewal rates will be low.

For associations, a successful health plan will produce a stream of income benefiting the association and tied to the number of participating employees in the plan. The more employees who subscribe to the plan through their employers, the more non-dues revenue the plan will generate for the Association. This serves as a check on the plan tying the financial success of the venture to the actual utility and satisfaction of the member and its employees.

For employers, a successful health plan will deliver promised upfront premium savings, predictably low renewal rates, ease of implementation and management, and lower employee turnover. The more that a business' employees recognize the value in their employer sponsored benefits, the less likely those employees are to leave one job for another without comparable benefits. Less employee turnover and lower overall health insurance premium spend mean more money to the bottom line for the business.

For employees, a successful health plan provides easy and affordable access to the healthcare system. Employees are tired of paying for health insurance where utilizing the benefits in the plan are cost-prohibitive. High deductibles, copays, and out-of-pocket maximums, low coinsurance percentages, and sheaves of paperwork to complete turn a plan meant for an employee's benefit into a hassle.

Employees expect support from their employers for health care expenses, and will leave an otherwise fulfilling position to get it. In fact, those who are unsatisfied with their health benefits are 20 percent more likely to look for other work. Low upfront premium costs and generous plan design allow employees to access their healthcare benefits more frequently and at less long-term cost than a traditional fully-insured plan allows. When this happens,employee satisfaction is high, they value both the benefit and the employer providing it.

Professional Associations around the country are embracing association-based health plans as a way to increase relevancy and usefulness for their member-employers. Any association not investigating an association-based health plan to assist its members in controlling healthcare costs for their employees should reexamine both its decision and its commitment to its members. By providing lower upfront premium costs, predictably lower renewal rates, innovative, flexible and inclusive plan designs, and high stakeholder satisfaction these associations are solving real business problems for their members. Employers are well-advised to spend their membership budget dollars in associations who have launched an association-based health plan to garner these benefits for themselves.

TREY TAYLOR

CEO

Taylor Insurance Services
Valdosta, GA

Trey is the Chief Executive Officer of Taylor Insurance Services. Trey holds a Bachelor's degree in History from Emory University in Atlanta, a Juris Doctor degree in Tax and Corporate Transactions from Tulane University and has done post-graduate work at the Kellogg School of Management at Northwestern University and the Georgia Institute of Technology. He is the Author of five books including *A CEO Only Does Three Things.*

www.taylorinsuranceservices.com
trey@rtaylorins.com
229.247.6411

TOM DORYWALSKI

Vice President of Business Development
Taylor Insurance Services
Valdosta, GA

Tom is the Vice President of Business Development for Taylor Insurance Services where he leads the firm's efforts in the health and wellness space. Tom received his Bachelor's degree in Business from Florida International University in Miami. He as advised dozens of Professional Associations in the launch of association-based health plans and is a frequent speaker on the topic.

www.taylorinsuranceservices.com
tdorywalski@rtaylorins.com
229.247.6411

NextGeneration Healthcare
CONCLUSION

T he time for NextGeneration Healthcare is here! This book has pulled back the curtain on some of the most powerful concepts, strategies, and solutions your organization can (should) leverage to take back control of the ever-rising costs of healthcare.

Imagine being able to reduce your healthcare budget by 20 to 40 or more in the next 12 months . . .

Imagine providing a better, more comprehensive experience for your employees so they are happier, healthier, and more productive . . .

Imagine how your organization could reallocate the vast savings created from managing the Healthcare Value Chain . . .

There's no reason to merely accept premium cost increases year after year from insurance companies who have a vested interest in conflict with yours. Instead, you now have the understanding and tools required to not only push back against the status quo, but actually move beyond it where you have control and incentives are properly aligned amongst your organization, your employees, your NextGen Benefits Adviser, and the healthcare providers.

To achieve these results, change is required, and it is not always easy or fast. However, by engaging the right adviser who understands how to properly manage the Healthcare Value Chain, you're organization will likely be able to experience meaningful results very quickly.

To ensure you are empowered to take action on what you've learned in these pages, here is a simple three step process to get you moving in the right direction now:

Step 1: Review Key Concepts

Go back and reread the parts of the book that resonated with you and your organization the most. Of course, not every strategy or solution is a fit for every group, so identify those ideas and methods that you think could benefit your company the fastest and easiest.

Step 2: Engage a NextGeneration Benefits Adviser

One of the most critical activities you can complete is finding the right NextGen Benefits Adviser who not only understands the concepts in this book, but can effectively implement them for your organization. (Note: understand that often it will be the smaller advisory firms who will be the most effective, because the business model of the larger national firms is dependent upon the status quo of misaligned incentives.)

Step 3: Commit to Moving Beyond "Healthcare as Usual"

In order for your organization to truly see the effect of Healthcare Value Chain management strategies, there first must be a commitment from the strategic leaders (often those at the S-Suite level) to no longer accept a perverse and unsustainable status quo of ever-increasing healthcare costs. Without such a commitment and mandate from the top, an organization is unlikely to make the important and valuable changes to actually make things better.

This simple three step process will empower you and your organization to move forward and create the astonishing financial and personnel benefits and results of NextGeneration Healthcare.

Empower Your Organization
to Break Through the Status Quo
of Skyrocketing Healthcare Costs!

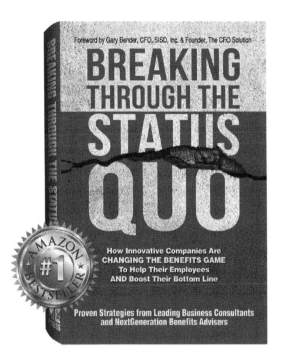

Get your copy of this Amazon bestselling and game-changing book written to help employers navigate the healthcare system to help their employees while also driving savings to the bottom line.

Read the Foreword from *Breaking Through The Status Quo* on the following pages.

FOREWORD

from *Breaking Through The Status Quo*

To any Chief Financial Officer or other C-level executive, *Breaking Through The Status Quo* is a MUST read. I can't be any more emphatic. If you want to understand why your benefits spend is both sky-high and seemingly out of control, you *must* read this book. If you want to know how you can seize control of your benefits spend, you *must* read this book. And if you want to begin to control the cost drivers to reduce your benefits spend without reducing the quality of your benefits, you *must* read this book.

As a CFO myself, I know the frustration and sense of powerlessness as year after year the HR department brings annual increases (often double digit) in the benefits budget, accompanied by earnest assurances that "This really is the best we could do" or "We're fortunate that our increase is below national trend!" Inquire deeper of your broker or consultant and you're told, "There's not much we can do. You're at the mercy of medical trend" or "We have influence with the insurance carrier but, in the end, it's up to the actuaries." So we've learned to settle—and be grateful—for a "less bad" renewal increase.

Read this book and you'll finally discover for yourself the exciting and empowering truth I recently discovered from my own benefits adviser, a NextGeneration Benefits Adviser who is one of the authors of this book.

I learned that I CAN control my benefits spend; that I DO have the power to reduce the cost of my employees' healthcare; and that I CAN offer affordable, sustainable benefits without shifting cost to my employees or cutting their benefits.

I also realized—and you will, too, if you read this book— that status quo brokers, which is most of them, have treated CFOs and CEOs like mushrooms...they've kept us in the dark and fed us a steady diet of manure. These status quo brokers are not bad people; they just have misaligned incentives that keep them from exploring alternatives to the status quo...because, frankly, the status quo works for them. It just doesn't work for me or other business leaders who offer employee benefits.

I should point out that my interest in the strategies in this book derives from more than just my professional responsibilities as a CFO. I'm also the founder of The CFO Solution, an organization whose mission is to help you, the private company CFO, by conveying proven best practices that solve problems for your company and introducing you to proven, better partners to execute these best practices.

With the CFO Solution, I'm committed to identifying

proven and cutting-edge solutions to the big problems facing the C-Suite today. And few problems rise to the level of the typical corporate benefits budget, whose unchecked but unpredictable growth is choking off employee pay raises and creating huge uncertainty in the business planning process.

Breaking Through The Status Quo is almost a one-stop shop for proven solutions for employee benefits and the benefits spend. And, frankly, it's not rocket science. My adviser and this book make plain that the real problem with employee benefits is that we in the C-Suite simply have not treated our benefits like we do every other key part of our business.

Fiduciary oversight? Yes, of every business unit in the company...except benefits. Executive management? Yes, of every business unit in the company...except benefits. Supply chain management? Of course, for every single business unit in the company...except benefits.

My adviser and the other authors of this book are bringing these essential business practices to our benefits budget and our employees' healthcare spend. They are working with the CFO to ensure fiduciary oversight, shifting the strategic decision-making on the benefits budget from HR to the C-Suite to engage executive management, and providing supply chain management to the employees' healthcare to promote appropriate utilization of medical services and plan resources.

As a CFO, this just makes perfect sense to me. So, in a way, what's been missing from my benefits process—and what my NextGeneration Benefits Adviser is working to get into the process is—me, as CFO. What's missing from your benefits process, then, is you, as the CFO or CEO of your company.

And, just as I don't do supply chain management for my other business units, I don't have to with benefits. That's what my benefits adviser does. And does well.

My adviser has helped me lower my costs dramatically AND has improved our benefits. We recently had him as our guest speaker at a CFO Solution forum and the attendees, both the CFOs and their HR teams, were impressed and anxious to engage!

My adviser has found EBITDA trapped in my benefits budget and he's helping me get it out and back on my bottom line where it belongs, which he's done for other of his clients. That's a terrific result that I'm quite excited about.

If the idea of converting part of your benefits spend into EBITDA appeals to you, if the idea of taking control of your benefits spend appeals to you, if the idea of reducing healthcare costs while improving your benefits appeals to you...you'll love the strategies in this book. So, like I said, you MUST read this book.

—**Gary Bender,** CFO
SISD, Inc.
Founder, The CFO Solution
www.thecfosolution.org

About AIL Press

AIL Press is the publishing division of the Association for Insurance Leadership—an organization committed to elevating the employee benefits industry by helping advisers become more effective and valuable to their clients. Through publications like this book as well as other programming, AIL Press strives to bring new, meaningful insights to the marketplace.

Learn more at: **www.AIL-Assn.org**